FAILURE IS IMPOSSIBLE!

FAILURE IS IMPOSSIBLE!
The History of American Women's Rights

MARTHA E. KENDALL

LERNER PUBLICATIONS COMPANY • MINNEAPOLIS

This book is dedicated to everyone, past and present, who has furthered women's progress in America.

Many thanks to the following people who helped make failure impossible as I wrote and rewrote this book: Pat Compton; Joan Cottle; Mary Eckhart; Donna Guthrie; Joy Hulme; Roz Kay; Jan Stiles; my entire family; and Sara Saetre, my always enthusiastic editor at Lerner.

Lerner Publications Company
A division of Lerner Publishing Group
241 First Avenue North
Minneapolis, MN 55401 U.S.A.

Website address: www.lernerbooks.com

Library of Congress Cataloging-in-Publication Data

Kendall, Martha E.
    Failure is impossible! : the history of American women's rights / by Martha E. Kendall.
      p. cm. — (People's history)
    Includes bibliographical references and index.
      ISBN 0-8225-1744-2 (lib. bdg. : alk. paper)
      1. Women—United States—History—Juvenile literature. 2. Women's rights—United States—History—Juvenile literature. [1. Women's rights—History. 2. Feminism—History.] I. Title. II. Series.
    HQ1121.K456 2001
    305.42'0973—dc21   00-009707

Manufactured in the United States of America
1 2 3 4 5 6 – JR – 06 05 04 03 02 01

Contents

A Note to Readers *7*

God's Hand Is Seen *8*

Remember the Ladies *18*

A Chain of Oppressions *28*

Setting the Ball in Motion *38*

Never Give In, Never Give Up *48*

From Aprons to Overalls—and Back *66*

Sisterhood Is Powerful *76*

Remarkable Women *86*

Timeline *90*

Selected Bibliography *92*

Further Reading *93*

Index *94*

A NOTE TO READERS

In the past, many people who researched women's struggle for equality focused only on suffrage—women's right to vote. But a complete view of women's rights includes much more. From colonial times in the early 1600s and through much of the 1800s, women fought for the right to keep their own wages, sign contracts, give speeches, own property, and retain custody of their children after their husband's death.

For generations, women could not become doctors or lawyers. They were paid less than men and had fewer opportunities for promotion. Their education was also limited. In fact, not until 1972 and the passage of Title IX of the Higher Education Act were public schools ordered to provide equal athletic opportunities for girls and boys. That legislation resulted in a spectacular increase in girls' and women's participation in sports during the last quarter of the twentieth century.

In the early 1970s, American historians began expanding the study of women's rights to include far more than the suffrage movement. They researched old court cases, autobiographies, newspaper accounts, and other public documents as well as personal journals, letters, and diaries. As a result, the story of American women's rights and roles began to be understood and told in greater detail.

In writing *Failure Is Impossible!*, I drew on this growing wealth of material. I described famous leaders of the women's movement, but I also included a great deal about ordinary, little-known individuals who advanced the progress of women. Rights were won not only in the limelight of national politics but also on public playgrounds and in private parlors, in cotton fields and in corporate offices.

It is my hope that in the following pages the lives of our foremothers emerge from the shadows of U.S. history. These women have contributed to the story of Americans claiming equal rights to "life, liberty, and the pursuit of happiness." In describing the accomplishments of women of the past, I am reminded of the debt we owe them all—and the work they began that remains to be completed.

—Martha E. Kendall

GOD'S HAND IS SEEN

I am no witch. I am innocent. I know nothing of it.
— Bridget Bishop, before her execution for the crime of witchcraft, Salem, Massachusetts, 1692

During the mid-1600s, in the small community of Boston in what was then Massachusetts Bay Colony, a housewife complained in public about a carpenter who had done some work in her home. According to her, he'd done a bad job and overcharged her to boot. Several centuries later, such a pronouncement would hardly create a stir. But Ann Hibbens must have been aware that women in her community were supposed to let their husbands manage family affairs. According to Christian teachings, he should have been the one to speak out.

Leaders of the Puritan church in Boston scolded Hibbens, saying she had acted "as if she were able to manage it better than her husband, which is a plain breach of the rule of Christ." Ann Hibbens appeared again in public records in 1656, when she was executed for being a witch.

During the last half of the seventeenth century, more than three hundred women in New England were accused of witchcraft. No one knows exactly how many were put to death, but estimates put the number close to fifty.

About twenty men were accused of witchcraft, too. But more women were accused since most people believed women were more likely to be witches. The devil found it easier to corrupt the souls of the "weaker sex." Many of the women charged with witchcraft were strong-willed, like Ann Hibbens, or unmarried, childless, or successful—all characteristics that did not fit the Puritan idea of femininity.

The persecution of women as witches, which continued until the end of the 1600s, is perhaps the most striking, but not the only, example of the lack of women's rights in the American colonies.

Opposite, *a Massachusetts Bay Colony woman stands trial for witchcraft.* **Right,** *in this illustration of life in the 1600s, New England colonists arrest an old woman accused of being a witch. The persecution of women as witches led to the deaths of at least twenty-four people in Salem, Massachusetts, in 1692.*

Colonial women were expected to tend to domestic tasks such as cleaning and to "give way" to the authority of their husbands. They were excluded from church leadership and civil government.

SPINSTERS AND THE RULE OF THUMB

"She eateth not the bread of idleness." So boasted one proud colonial American husband of his dutiful wife. On a typical day, she tended the orchard, made cider and cheese, baked bread and pies, served meals to family and guests, sewed and knitted, washed and ironed clothes, and cleaned the house.

Colonial American women were also kept busy with large families. As many as twelve or thirteen children (some of them born of previous marriages in which one parent had died) lived under one roof. Additional youngsters, such as orphaned cousins, sometimes joined a family.

Although colonial women played an essential role in these households, the spiritual and customary head of the family was the father. Colonists followed teachings of the Bible such as "The head of the woman is the man" and "Wives, be in subjection to your own husbands." John Robinson, a pastor in Plymouth Colony, described the process of decision-making in a marriage this way: "Differences will arise and be seen, and so the one must give way.... This, God and nature layeth upon the woman, rather than upon the man."

Popular books also promoted this division of roles. *Lady's New Year's Gift, or, Advice to a Daughter,* published in London in 1688, became a bestseller in the American colonies. Its author, George Savile, claimed that men were more intelligent and logical than women. As he put it, men "have the larger share of reason." Therefore, according to Savile (and to many colonists), men needed to be in charge of businesses, families, and other enterprises. Since a woman clearly needed a husband, Savile warned women who were not happily married to "make the best of it."

Not surprisingly, the colonies had few unmarried women. Life was not easy for those who did remain single. They had few opportunities to earn a living, so their parents, a brother, or a married sister provided food and lodging and covered other expenses for them. To earn their keep in the home of a relative, most single women helped to care for their relatives' children and took on many household tasks. Single women spent so many hours at the time-consuming and tedious task of spinning that they came to be called "spinsters."

Laws and customs tied a wife's money to her husband—just as if she had tied her apron around him. Although the situation varied from colony to colony and from decade to decade, most often a wife could not make contracts and could not own property. A husband could use or sell any of the couple's possessions as he saw fit. If a woman had any money as a single woman, it became her husband's when she married. She had no legal right to wages she earned. If a husband fell into debt, his creditors could seize his wife's belongings

Single women in the colonies were called "spinsters," because they usually lived with relatives and earned their keep by doing the most tedious tasks, such as spinning.

for payment. If he died, he could leave property—even property that had originally been hers—to anyone. Thus a husband had the power of what came to be called "the apron-string hold." One of the few laws that protected women gave a widow at least one-third of a couple's property after her husband's death.

A couple's children were considered the husband's. Divorce in colonial America was rare, but when it did happen, the father had the right to sole custody of the children. In a husband's will, he could direct that, in the event of his death, custody of the children be granted to someone other than their mother.

Laws also allowed a husband to physically discipline his wife. He could whip her as long as the whip he used was not thicker than his thumb. This rule came to be known as the "rule of thumb." During colonial times, the rule of thumb was likely seen not as an oppression of women, but as an assertion of their right not to be beaten too severely.

If a wife ran away from home, a husband could petition a colonial court to force her to return to him. One court ordered that a wife "either repair to her husband with all convenient speed . . . or . . . give a reason why shee doth not." The punishment for disobeying an order to reconcile was banishment from the colony. Many husbands of runaway wives advertised in local papers, asking for information about the whereabouts of the escapee. Sometimes a husband declared that his runaway wife had stolen goods from him—such as her clothes.

Sometimes colonial courts recognized contracts made before a marriage that safeguarded a woman's rights after her marriage. When John Phillips and Faith Doty married in 1667 in Plymouth Colony,

Everything in a colonial woman's home—including her child and her own clothes—legally belonged to her husband.

they signed an agreement promising Faith, a widow, would retain "all her house and land, goods and cattles, that she is now possessed of, to her owne proper use, to dispose of them att her owne free will from time to time, and att any time, as shee shall see cause." Without such a prenuptial contract, Faith would have kept no legal interest in property she had acquired together with her late first husband.

"I CAST YOU OUT"

One of the most famous women of early colonial America was Anne Hutchinson. Anne and her husband, William, were Puritans. In 1634 they had left England, where Puritans were persecuted, to immigrate to the "New World" of North America so that they could worship freely.

When they arrived in Boston with their eleven children, however, they discovered that true freedom of religion did not exist there. The same men who established rules for the church also governed the colony. Questioning Puritan rules was the same as questioning the laws of the colony and the authority of its leaders. The church taught that only ministers could understand what God wanted people to do.

Puritan congregations strictly enforced church teachings, excommunicating those who rebelled. This was a stern punishment, since most people believed that church membership was essential for achieving salvation—going to heaven after death. Church teachings were even more confining for women than for men. Wives were to obey their husbands in all things. In church, women were to sit apart from the men and remain silent.

The church also taught that a life full of good works was the only path to salvation. Anne Hutchinson certainly led a life of good works. She nursed the sick, delivered babies, and diligently tended her children and home. But her religious beliefs differed from those of church leaders. She was an antinomian—a person who believes that people are saved through faith alone.

Anne Hutchinson preached in her home. Governor John Winthrop said that even though Hutchinson had not "bine unfaythfull" to her husband, unfaithfulness was sure to follow improper behavior such as preaching. He forbade it.

Hutchinson began opening her home on Sunday evenings, inviting women to come to hear her speak about her beliefs. Word spread about her lively talks, and sometimes as many as eighty women crowded into her small parlor. To accommodate everyone, she added a second weekly meeting. Soon men began attending, too. Hutchinson also began speaking in neighboring communities.

Puritan women were not allowed to teach religion, and Hutchinson was not only teaching religion but also gaining in popularity. The Puritan leaders in the area began looking on her actions with alarm. "If [women] be allowed in one thing," declared John Winthrop, governor of the colony, "[they] must be admitted a rule in all things; for they being above reason and Scripture, they are not subject to control." Another influential man, Hugh Peter, warned Hutchinson, "You have stepped out of your place, you have been a husband rather than a wife, and a preacher rather than a hearer."

Despite repeated warnings, Anne Hutchinson did not stop her religious teaching. In late 1638, the Massachusetts Bay Colony arrested her for the crime of disorderly meeting. According to Winthrop, "Though women might meet (some few together) to pray . . . , where sixty or more did meet every week . . . was agreed to be disorderly." A trial was set to be heard before the General Court of Massachusetts to determine whether Anne Hutchsinon should be excommunicated and banished from the colony. She was then forty-six years old and pregnant with her sixteenth baby.

At the trial, Winthrop, who acted as judge, accused Hutchinson of breaking the fifth commandment of the Bible: "Honor thy father and mother." She exclaimed that she had done no such thing. The words *father* and *mother*, he answered, meant anyone in authority, so Hutchinson had broken the commandment by refusing to obey church leaders.

As the trial continued, Winthrop cited many Bible passages to try to show the ways Hutchinson had betrayed God's laws. Time after time, she responded with a Bible passage that countered his point. Eventually Winthrop cut off the debate, saying, "We do not mean to discourse with those of your sex." He pronounced his verdict: "I cast you out and deliver you to Satan . . . . You are to be imprisoned till the court shall send you away."

In March 1639, after four months in prison, Anne Hutchinson was released but forced to leave the colony. She, her family, and thirty-five other families left Boston. A rugged weeklong trip northward through wilderness brought them all to the newly established colony of Rhode Island, a place of greater religious freedom.

Rhode Island proved to be a temporary refuge, however. Winthrop annexed it, bringing it under his authority. Then William Hutchinson died. Fearing renewed persecution, Anne Hutchinson fled to a Dutch settlement in modern New York state. A few months later, Native Americans, at war with European settlers in the region, raided the settlement. Anne Hutchinson and five of her children were killed. When John Winthrop heard the news, he declared, "God's hand is . . . seen herein."

REMEMBER THE LADIES

Remember, all men would be tyrants if they could.
—Abigail Smith Adams, writing to her husband, future U.S. president John Adams, 1776

For decades in the 1700s, Great Britain struggled against France to dominate North America. By the mid-1760s, Great Britain ruled thirteen colonies on the continent and controlled miles of mostly unsettled land in British Canada. Britain began passing a series of laws that were unpopular in the colonies. They imposed high taxes on colonists, despite the fact that colonists were not represented in the British government. In 1776 the colonies brazenly submitted a Declaration of Independence from Great Britain and its king, George III. The result was war.

Most American patriots who took up arms against the British were men; custom forbade women from joining the patriots' Continental army. A few women joined anyway. One was Deborah Sampson. She disguised herself by cutting her hair short and wearing men's clothing; she then enlisted in the army under the name Timothy Thayer. Despite her precautions, her identity was soon discovered, and she was dismissed.

Determined to be part of the action, Sampson enlisted again, this time as Robert Shurtleff. She spent the next three years in the infantry, fighting in battle after battle beside her male comrades. Once, she caught a musket ball in her thigh. In the course of removing it, a surgeon probably would have discovered her sex, so she removed the bullet herself.

After the war, as many patriot soldiers were being congratulated on their victory, Deborah Sampson's exploits became known. Her church

Opposite, *Abigail Adams.* **Above,** *Deborah Sampson disguised herself as a man to fight as a patriot during the American Revolution.*

expelled her for her "unchristian" behavior. Sampson acknowledged that she had "swerved from the accustomed flowery path of female delicacy." Although her participation in the revolt against Great Britain had been indelicate by the standards of her time, it had also helped establish a new nation. In addition, Deborah Sampson demonstrated her own revolt against the limited options available to women.

"LAWS IN WHICH WE HAVE NO VOICE"

Among the people who created the new United States government were George Washington, John Adams, and Benjamin Franklin. These men and the nation's other founding fathers rejected the belief, widely held in Europe, that kings and queens rule by divine, or God-given, right. Instead, American patriots adopted the radical notion that "all men are created equal." This idea, some hoped, might eventually free all nations from the rule of kings and queens.

Abigail Smith Adams, the wife of John Adams, wrote to him as he met with the other founders in Philadelphia, Pennsylvania, to chart a government for the new nation. She compared the rule of kings over their subjects to the rule of men over their wives:

> I desire you would remember the ladies and be more generous and favorable to them than your ancestors. Do not put such unlimited power into the hands of the husbands. Remember, all men would be tyrants if they could. If particular care and attention is not paid to the ladies, we . . . will not hold ourselves bound by any laws in which we have no voice or representation.

She argued that the finest husbands "willingly give up the harsh title of master for the more tender and endearing one of friend." Therefore, only the most tyrannical husbands would benefit from laws favoring men. "Why . . . not put it out of the power of the vicious . . . to use us with cruelty?" she asked.

He replied, "As to your extraordinary code of laws, I cannot but laugh."

In fact, the phrase "all men are created equal" referred only to some men: white males who owned property. When the U.S. Constitution was finished, it gave only white, propertied men the right to vote and to hold public office.

Abigail Adams told her husband, "I cannot say that I think you are very generous to the ladies; for, whilst you are . . . emancipating all nations, you insist upon retaining an absolute power over wives." And in a letter to a friend written in 1776, John Adams acknowledged that the new nation would "govern women without their consent."

In 1791—about six years before John Adams became president of the United States—the First Amendment to the U.S. Constitution was passed. It strictly separated religion and government. The amendment was not enacted in order to advance women's rights, but perhaps Anne Hutchinson would have seen its passage as a step forward nonetheless.

NO MASTER TO DRIVE US

Native American women in early America generally enjoyed more rights within their tribes than women of European descent enjoyed within their communities. For example, within an alliance of northeastern tribes called the Iroquois League of Nations, children belonged to their mother's clan, not to their father's. The elder women of each clan controlled the sale of land. When the clan's men planned a raid against a distant tribe, the women supplied the food the warriors would need for the journey. If the women disapproved of the raid, they vetoed it by refusing to supply the food.

Iroquois women also selected a clan's new chiefs. If a chief proved lacking, the women removed his horned headdress as a symbol that they were removing his power. Once the women had "knocked off a chief's horns," he was relegated to the ranks of the warriors.

The Seneca were one tribe within the Iroquois League of Nations. One twelve-year-old white girl, Mary Jemison, was captured by members of the Seneca. Mary's parents and most of her siblings were killed.

Many years later, when Jemison was eighty years old, writer James Seaver interviewed her and told her story in his book *A Narrative of the Life of Mrs. Mary Jemison,* published in 1824. In the book, Jemison told how she had married a Seneca man and raised a large family in western New York state. Shortly after the American Revolution, she had been given the chance to return to her original home. But she was happy with the Seneca and had chosen to remain with them. One of the main reasons for Jemison's contentment, she said, was the freedom Seneca women enjoyed. Compared to white women, the Seneca women's "cares certainly are not half as numerous, nor as great." Seneca women, she explained, had "no master to oversee or drive us."

"THE MARKET OF MARRIAGE"

Throughout the 1700s, most women did not work outside the home. Almost all professions and occupations were closed to women. Women's jobs were strictly reserved for women. Most were low-paying jobs such as maid, cook, or laundress.

A portrait of Iroquois woman Rant-Che-Wai-We. Iroquois women enjoyed equal status with Iroquois men.

Young girls in the 1700s were carefully prepared for the roles they would assume later as wives and mothers. Even small girls wore adult fashions such as these corseted gowns.

Consequently, marriage and money meant pretty much the same thing to most women. Widows and single women, called "solitaries," sometimes could not afford homes of their own. Instead, they had to live with a married brother or sister. As *New York* magazine put it in 1797, marriage for many was the "sole method of procuring for themselves an establishment."

To prepare for marriage, most girls spent their time doing practical things such as cooking, sewing, and taking care of other household chores. Since many people considered the Bible's teachings essential, both boys and girls needed to be able to read it. But academic subjects beyond reading were not necessary for most girls, whose future responsibilities would lie within the home.

Middle- and upper-class girls who studied subjects beyond the ba-
sics were often taught social skills such as music and dancing, appro-
priate topics for the delicate feminine mind. Perhaps most important,
young women learned to be fashionable. In a childhood journal,
Frances Willard described the day she first had to look like a lady.
"Mother insists that at last I must have my hair 'done up woman-
fashion.' She says she can hardly forgive herself for letting me 'run
wild' so long . . . . My 'back' hair is twisted up like a corkscrew; I
carry eighteen hair-pins; my head aches miserably; my feet are entan-
gled in the skirt of my hateful new gown. I can never jump over a
fence again, so long as I live."

Having been carefully groomed to be attractive to the opposite sex,
many young women were expected to marry well. They often evalu-
ated marriage proposals based on a man's financial situation. In a letter to her cousin, wealthy Eliza Southgate wrote, "Not one woman in
a hundred marries for love." Southgate preferred not to marry, since
that would put her under the control of a husband. "I had rather be
the meanest reptile that creeps the earth," she wrote, "than live a slave
to the despotic [all-powerful] will of another."

Southgate echoed the sentiments of Mary Wollstonecraft's book *A
Vindication of the Rights of Woman,* which was published in Great
Britain in 1792 and reprinted in Philadelphia soon after. The uncon-
ventional Wollstonecraft declared, "The divine right of husbands, like
the divine right of kings, may, it is to be hoped, in this enlightened
age be contested without danger." One American woman who read
Wollstonecraft's book proclaimed, "She speaks my mind." But Timothy Dwight, future president of Yale, later ridiculed Wollstonecraft,
calling her "a strumpet" (a woman of poor character) because, although she had born a child, she had chosen not to marry.

MOTHERS IN A DEMOCRACY

Although many marriage customs continued unchanged after the
American Revolution, many people began to believe that wives and

In her 1792 book **A Vindication of the Rights of Woman,** *Mary Wollstonecraft declared, "I do earnestly wish to see the distinction of sex abolished altogether . . . save where love is concerned."*

mothers had a new role to play. Mothers had always guided their children and often taught them to read. Now they needed to take a stronger role in educating their children.

One well-known physician, Benjamin Rush, led a small but influential group of men in the early 1800s who said that a broader education for girls would prepare them for life in democracy. Better-educated girls could one day teach their children to "think justly upon the great subject of liberty and government," wrote Rush. After all, women were rearing sons who must know how to be good citizens and how to rule themselves. The Young Ladies Academy in Philadelphia, Pennsylvania, founded in 1786, reflected this philosophy.

Another early school to offer a high-school level curriculum to girls was the Troy Female Seminary in Troy, New York. Founded by Emma Willard in 1821, the school taught girls the arts and such "masculine" subjects as English composition and physical exercise. Emma Willard agreed with Benjamin Rush that the purpose of educating girls was to improve their effectiveness as mothers.

Thus even the most forward-thinking educators did not consider that an education might prepare girls for active lives in the world

The Troy Female Seminary in Troy, New York

beyond the home. Graduates of Emma Willard's seminary who chose not to marry could become schoolteachers, a profession open to them because of its similarity to a mother's teaching role.

But the late 1700s and early 1800s held few other career options for girls. Priscilla Mason, who graduated as a salutatorian of the Young Ladies Academy, spoke about this lack of options in an address she made at her commencement. She praised her opportunity for schooling. But in an unusually strong protest against limitations on women, she also pointed out that "the Church, the Bar [the legal profession] and the Senate are shut against us."

Writer Judith Sargent Murray was one of several women who contributed articles to newspapers in this era. Using the pen name Constantia, Murray wrote an article in 1790 entitled "On the Equality of the Sexes." Published in *Massachusetts Magazine,* it proclaimed that male domination stemmed from "the difference of education and continued advantages." Like men, she argued, women needed to know how to survive on their own—and they had the right to earn needed money. Girls "should be enabled to procure for themselves the necessaries of life," Murray proclaimed; "independence should be placed within their grasp." Murray herself enjoyed a good education because as a child in Gloucester, Massachusetts, she had been allowed to listen while her brother was tutored for entrance to Harvard.

Frances Wright, an immigrant to the United States from Scotland, believed that education was the key to giving girls more than the choice of marriage or poverty. Wright gave public speeches—something conventional women did not do. Teaching daughters nothing but a little music and dancing and giving them a few fine gowns, she charged, prepared them for nothing but "the market of marriage." Wright claimed that if she had not been made to conform to women's fashions, she would have become "ten times more of a person."

"We see men who will aid the instruction of their sons, and condemn only their daughters to ignorance," she declared. "'Our sons,' they say, 'will have to exercise political rights, may aspire to public offices, may fill some learned profession.' But 'for our daughters,' they say—if indeed respecting them they say any thing—'for our daughters, little trouble or expense is necessary. They can never be any thing; in fact, they are nothing.'"

A CHAIN OF OPPRESSIONS

Oh men with sisters dear,
Oh men with mothers and wives,
It is not linen
you're wearing out,
It's human creatures' lives.
—handbill printed by the Shirt
     Sewers of New York, 1851

While Judith Sargent Murray, Mary Wollstonecraft, Frances Wright, and others urged women to become better educated than their forebears had been, other people—including many women—hotly debated the need. Some of them argued that an educated woman would develop masculine traits such as ambition and would drive male suitors away. In 1829 Catharine Beecher cautioned girls against gaining too much knowledge. "The moment woman begins to feel the promptings of ambition, or the thirst for power," Beecher wrote, "her aegis of defence [source of protection] is gone." Ironically, Beecher's words appeared in a book she called *Suggestions Respecting Improvements in Education.*

Beecher's words reflected a notion that was widely promoted in the 1830s, an idea of what a "proper" lady is like. Magazines such as the hugely popular *Godey's Lady's Book* offered women advice on how to behave and how to exert a wholesome moral influence on their families. *Godey's* also offered illustrations of the latest fashions: long, sweeping skirts so wide that a woman could hardly fit through a doorway and tight corsets that made her waist look tiny. *Godey's* seemed to say that a lady stayed home, supervised the servants who took care of her house and children, and did as little other work as possible. Her dress proved that she was idle (she couldn't work in it). She was obviously supported by a father, husband, or brother who could afford to keep her as a lovely ornament. This view of women as affluent, pampered creatures came to be called "the cult of true womanhood."

Yet many women found that they could not necessarily rely on a man. The cult of true womanhood did not fit with the realities of their lives. In Elizabeth Cady Stanton's autobiography, *Eighty Years*

In the 1800s, magazines such as **Godey's Lady's Book** *illustrated the latest fashions with drawings, not photographs. Here a woman models a ball gown that exaggerates her tiny waist and creates the impression that she has a delicate constitution.*

and More, she included a story from her childhood in Johnstown, New York, in the 1820s. A local woman named Flora Campbell lived with her husband on a farm that had belonged to Flora's parents. When Flora's husband died, he willed the farm to the couple's son. The son then made his mother leave.

Wondering what her rights might be, Flora Campbell turned to little Elizabeth's father, Daniel Cady, a lawyer. Elizabeth heard her father explain that under law a married woman's property belonged to her husband. He could will it to whomever he chose, and his heir could use the property in any way. Elizabeth thought that law was mean and decided to cut it out of her father's law books with a pair of scissors. Her father stopped her. If she wanted to change those laws, he said, she would have to go to the legislature.

MILL GIRLS

Throughout the nineteenth century, women found themselves saddled with what Lavinia Waight, secretary for the United Tailoresses Society of New York, called a "chain of oppressions against the truly dominated weaker sex." Waight charged that women were poorly paid, lacked opportunities for schooling, and were excluded from government, business, and other arenas in spite of their interests and talents. She demanded that the "lords and tyrants of the world" grant women equal opportunities.

Most women who worked in the early 1800s found wages pitifully low. In the late 1820s, a skilled tailor working in her home in New York City sewed from fifteen to sixteen hours a day to earn, on average, a dollar and a half a week. A woman who took in laundry might earn fifty cents to a dollar a week. That sum was not enough to live on.

Then in the late 1820s, huge textile mills and other factories began opening up. Women and girls flocked to them by the thousands, seeking jobs. "Mill girls" worked long days, from five in the morning until seven at night. They earned more money in the mills than they could in other jobs—sometimes as much as two dollars a week—but

Like this woman weaving on a mechanical loom, "mill girls" in the mid-1800s worked long days for low pay in the nation's new factories.

still found it hard to support themselves. Sometimes widows and other women who had no man to to support them worked in factories, but they still needed some charity, even if their children worked in the factories, too.

On average, female workers in any field in the early 1800s were paid one-fourth to one-half of what males earned for doing similar jobs. In the 1840s, the owner of a watch factory in Waltham, Massachusetts, applauded himself for paying women workers generously. He employed fifty women experienced in "tending the machines" and gave them four dollars a week. Men of similar experience in the same factory, however, made nearly three times as much.

The union to which Lavinia Waight belonged, the United Tailoresses Society of New York, was one of the first unions of women workers in the United States. In 1836 the union went on strike for higher wages. One of New York's most prominent newspapers, the New York Sun, made fun of the strike, urging women not to waste their time seeking better wages. Instead they should put their efforts into finding a husband. "We trust that they will render their strike more striking by exhibiting their striking beauties to the eyes of our sex, in a pretty procession round the Park," one article said. "It would . . . accomplish something more than a mere matter of money—say matrimony!" The strike failed, and eventually the union fell apart.

Also in 1836, mill workers in Lowell, Massachusetts, were told their wages were to be cut. Harriet Robinson was a worker at the mill and just eleven years old at the time. In a report she wrote years later for the Massachusetts Bureau of Statistics and Labor, she recalled, "When it was announced that the wages were to be cut down, great indignation was felt, and it was decided to strike or 'turn out' en masse."

So many of the Lowell workers did not show up for work that they successfully shut the mills down in what was the first massive strike in U.S. history. But again, the workers failed to force owners of the mills to raise wages. Workers called strikes at other factories in other cities, too, but almost all the strikes were defeated, and wages for all workers declined. The movement to unionize women workers continued long into the future, however.

Captured while fleeing from slavery, Margaret Garner killed two of her children rather than see them returned to a life of oppression.

LIVES OF SLAVE WOMEN

Perhaps the most glaring injustice in the chain of oppressions of women from the early 1600s onward was the fact that many American women were slaves. Life for them was even harder than for most white women. And they sometimes suffered in ways that male slaves did not. Not uncommonly, masters raped slave women. If a slave woman became pregnant, her child was a slave, regardless of who the father was. Sometimes masters sold mothers and their children to different owners, parting them forever.

One woman known only as Cornelia was born a slave on a small farm in Tennessee. As an old woman, she was interviewed about her early life and recalled how fiercely her mother, Fannie, had defended herself and her children. If Cornelia were ever faced with an unbearable demand, her mother told her she should fight. "And if you can't fight," she said, "kick; if you can't kick, then bite."

Fannie's master decided to send her away and ordered her to leave her tiny baby behind. "Ma took the baby by its feet . . . ," Cornelia recalled, "and with the baby's head swinging downward, she vowed to smash its brains out before she'd leave it. Tears were streaming down her face." In this case, a slave woman was able to influence her own fate. "It was seldom that Ma cried, and everyone knew that she meant every word," Cornelia said. "Ma took the baby with her."

Harriet Jacobs described her experiences in an autobiography called *Incidents in the Life of a Slave Girl*. Jacobs was born in the small town of Edenton, North Carolina, in 1813. When she was twelve years old, her mistress died, leaving Jacobs in her will to her three-year-old niece, Mary Norcom.

At the Norcoms', Mary's father, Dr. James Norcom, demanded sex from Harriet Jacobs. Jacobs continually had to fend him off. She wished she weren't attractive to him. "If God has bestowed beauty upon [a slave girl]," she wrote, "it will prove her greatest curse."

Unwilling to bear this situation, Jacobs slipped away one dark night in 1835. Because slaves were property, masters could take back escaping slaves, even if they fled to northern states where slavery was illegal. If Norcom caught Jacobs, he could torture her and possibly kill her. Norcom offered a three hundred dollar reward for Jacobs's return.

Jacobs had not fled far. She hid nearby in a tiny attic in a shed owned by her grandmother, a free black woman. She remained in hiding in the attic for seven years before she was able to escape by

Born a slave in North Carolina in 1813, Harriet Jacobs hid for seven years in an attic near her master's home before she was able to escape to the North and freedom.

sailing north on a ship whose captain was willing to harbor a runaway slave.

WOMEN AND ABOLITION

Many white people were enraged by the injustice of slavery and the particular wrongs done to slave women. For example, Sarah and Angelina Grimké were born into a wealthy slave-holding family in South Carolina in the early 1800s, but they both hated the slavery system. They moved to the North when they became adults and joined the abolition movement, which was demanding an end to slavery.

As the Grimké sisters worked in the abolition movement, they met many women who disapproved of slavery but did little to aid the efforts of abolitionists. Abolitionists were opposing slavery through public speaking, fundraising, and traveling door to door to gather signatures on petitions. All these activities were considered improper for "ladies."

In 1837 Catharine Beecher argued against women working publicly for abolition in her *Essay on Slavery and Abolitionism with Reference to the Duty of American Females.* She addressed the essay to

Angelina Grimké. In it, Beecher attacked women in political life. Then she praised some Boston, Massachusetts, ministers who had published a letter arguing that women should not participate publicly in the antislavery movement. Such participation, they said, would "threaten the female character with wide-spread and permanent injury." Women should restrict themselves to the home. "The power of women is in her dependence," they claimed.

Angelina Grimké had little respect for the reluctance of some women to do what she believed needed to be done. She wrote, "The denial of our duty to act, is a bold denial of our right to act; and if we have no right to act, then may we well be termed 'the white slaves of the North.'" Sarah Grimké agreed. "God created us equal," she declared. In a letter Sarah Grimké wrote to her sister in 1837, she said, "All I ask of our brethren is, that they will take their feet from off our necks and permit us to stand upright on the ground which God designed us to occupy."

The Grimké sisters—Angelina, left, and Sarah, right—protested both slavery and the restrictions that limited all women.

A cartoon in **Vanity Fair** *portrays abolitionists with exaggerated features and wearing ridiculous clothing. Angry bystanders pelt them with vegetables.*

In 1837 and 1838, Sarah and Angelina Grimké gave a series of lectures later published in *The New England Spectator* as "Letters on the Equality of the Sexes and the Condition of Woman." The articles pointed out that wives could not sign legal contracts. Women rarely received much education, which made them more vulnerable to the men who had authority over them. Since women, like slaves, had no legal identity apart from their husbands, their husbands were essentially "owners."

The connection between the condition of slaves and the condition of women made sense to many abolitionists. Despite opposition, women forged a partnership with the abolition movement that continued for several decades.

SETTING THE
BALL IN MOTION

We hold these truths to be self-evident, that all men and women are created equal.
—Elizabeth Cady Stanton, "Declaration of Sentiments," 1848

Elizabeth Cady Stanton long remembered the time Flora Campbell had been kicked off her farm and Mrs. Campbell had asked Mr. Cady about her property rights. That childhood memory influenced the remarkable path Elizabeth chose as a woman.

In 1832 she graduated from the Troy Female Seminary. It wasn't a college, but it was the best schooling a girl could get. She spent several years quietly, visiting friends and relatives often.

Then in 1840, she married abolitionist Henry Stanton. The newlyweds traveled to London, England, where Henry Stanton was to attend the first World Anti-Slavery Convention as a delegate from the American Anti-Slavery Society. At the convention, male delegates voted to bar female delegates from participating. The women had to sit behind a curtain and were not allowed to speak or vote. This made Elizabeth Cady Stanton furious. She and a delegate she met at the convention, Lucretia Mott, resolved to hold a women's rights convention when they returned to the United States.

The two exchanged letters for several years. Then in July 1848, Mott visited Waterloo, New York, not far from Stanton's home in Seneca Falls. Together with a small group of friends, the two women renewed their discussion about restrictions in women's lives. Women had gained some opportunity for higher education. In 1833 Oberlin College in Ohio had been the first college to open its doors to women. But most colleges did not admit women, and most jobs remained closed to women. Working women still earned less than half of what men earned for doing the same work.

Stanton and her friends also discussed temperance—the idea that the sale of liquor should be banned. Many people believed liquor was destroying families. If a woman tried to remove her children from a drunken father, she couldn't. The law gave custody to him.

Stanton inspired everyone at that gathering. They decided to publish a notice in the local newspaper the next day announcing a women's rights convention to be held in just five days. And Stanton began composing a "Declaration of Sentiments" to be read there.

COME TO SENECA FALLS

On July 19, 1848, more than two hundred women and about forty men made their way to the Wesleyan Chapel in Seneca Falls, New York. That was a large crowd, given the short notice. Stanton saw the significance not in their numbers but in their cause. "It was the most momentous reform that had yet been launched on the world," she wrote later.

Stanton had modeled her "Declaration of Sentiments" on the Declaration of Independence created by colonists in 1776. One injustice the colonists had rebelled against was "taxation without representation." Stanton pointed out that in 1848, women suffered the same injustice. Their wages were taxed, but they could not vote or be elected to office.

Stanton had never before spoken in public, but she read her declaration bravely. "We hold these truths to be self-evident, that all men *and women* are created equal." She declared, "Man has repeatedly denied woman her rights . . . He has never permitted her to vote. He has taken all her right to property and money."

Henry Stanton had refused to attend the convention. Twelve resolutions were being presented. One of them demanded woman suffrage—the right to vote. Henry Stanton was convinced that resolution would turn the convention into a joke. Lucretia Mott also thought that introducing the woman suffrage resolution was a bad idea. So many other rights, such as the right to joint guardianship of children, needed to be gained.

As the convention continued into July 20, people hotly debated the resolution regarding suffrage. Many agreed with Henry Stanton that woman suffrage was too radical an idea.

Then Frederick Douglass spoke. He was a free black man and one of the most famous speakers in the abolition movement. He himself could not vote because of his race. "The power to choose rules and make laws is the right by which all others can be secured," he pointed out. His support swayed just enough people. The convention barely adopted the woman suffrage resolution.

When reports of the convention appeared in newspapers around the nation, Henry Stanton's prediction proved true. Elizabeth Cady Stanton wrote, "All the journals from Maine to Texas seemed to strive with each other to see which could make our movement appear the most ridiculous." Some supporters began to distance themselves from the Seneca Falls convention.

Other people, such as Emily Collins of South Bristol, New York, were prompted to act. She gathered fifteen neighbors and formed a local equal rights society. All her life she had "pined for that freedom of thought and action that was then denied to all womankind . . . , " she wrote. "But not until that meeting at Seneca Falls in 1848 . . . did I take action." Soon women's rights reformers in many states began holding more conventions. Women's rights activists met in Rochester, New York; in New York City; and in towns in Ohio, Indiana, Massachusetts, and Pennsylvania. Topics at the conventions included not only woman suffrage but also reforms in education, property law, and the workplace.

STANTON AND ANTHONY

In 1851 Elizabeth Cady Stanton made a remarkable new friendship with Susan B. Anthony. Like Stanton, Anthony had discovered that reform movements would not let women participate fully—and she responded by organizing women. For example, the Sons of Temperance in New York State did not allow women to speak at their meetings. In 1852 Susan B. Anthony got Stanton to help her found the New York Women's State Temperance Society.

Anthony had worked tirelessly for both abolition and temperance, but the limitations for women were a constant source of frustration. Stanton encouraged her to shift her goals and work for women's rights. "We have other and bigger fish to fry," Stanton told Anthony in a letter.

Anthony heeded the advice, and the two became a team. Stanton had a large family, so she had little time to travel and lecture. Limiting her public speaking, she wrote stirring speeches from her home and published many magazine articles and pamphlets. Anthony, on the other hand, was single. She took on the role of traveling to speak, circulate petitions, and organize meetings. Sometimes Anthony visited Stanton and helped her with the children and the cooking so that Stanton could write. As Henry Stanton put it, "Susan stirred the puddings, Elizabeth stirred up Susan, and then Susan stirs up the world!"

Stirring up the world often meant reaching people like Emily Collins in scattered, small towns and then cultivating them as local women's rights leaders. Anthony told Stanton about a dinner she had had with the president of Oberlin College and his wife. After he had attacked women's rights advocates, his wife took Anthony aside. "You have the sympathy of a large proportion of the educated women with you," she told Anthony. "In my circle I hear the movement much talked of and earnest hopes for its spread expressed—but these women dare not speak out their sympathy." In the following years, Anthony showed a singular genius for finding and nurturing such hesitant supporters.

After the first women's rights conventions, few women's rights advocates ever again questioned whether women should vote. Instead the right to vote became their most important goal. The call for woman suffrage began to be heard across the nation. As Stanton put it, "We had set the ball in motion."

A FEW DISAPPOINTED WOMEN

As the women's rights movement got underway, advocates could see that the majority of people in the United States did not support its

Fast friends, Elizabeth Cady Stanton, **left,** *and Susan B. Anthony,* **right,** *joined forces in the fight for woman suffrage. Stanton coined the motto "Men, their rights and nothing more: women, their rights and nothing less."*

In plain language, Sojourner Truth was able to eloquently express the central issues of the women's rights movement of her time.

goals. One reason was that the people in the movement seemed to be challenging the cult of true womanhood.

Sojourner Truth, a former slave, could not read or write, but she traveled around the country, lecturing to thousands of people at anti-slavery and women's rights meetings. Both her life history as a slave and the fact that she gave public lectures contrasted sharply with the cult of true womanhood. At a women's rights convention in 1851, she responded to some hecklers who tried to disrupt the meeting by saying that women needed to be pampered and helped by men. Because she did not write down her speeches, no reliable written record of them exists. But Frances Gage, who attended the convention, reported Sojourner Truth's words this way:

> That man over there says that women need to be helped into carriages, and lifted over ditches, and to have the best place everywhere. Nobody ever helps me into carriages, or over mud-puddles, or gives me any best place! And ain't I a woman? Look at me! Look at my arm! I have ploughed and planted,

and gathered into barns, and no man could head me! And ain't I a woman? I could work as much and eat as much as a man—when I could get it—and bear the lash as well! And ain't I a woman? I have borne thirteen children, and seen them most all sold off to slavery, and when I cried out with my mother's grief, none but Jesus heard me! And ain't I a woman?

Another example of resistance to women's rights came when some women challenged restrictive fashions. In 1851 Elizabeth Cady Stanton's cousin designed some baggy, ankle-length trousers—the first pants meant for women. The trousers were worn under a skirt that was shortened to just above the knee. Instead of lifting a huge skirt when crossing muddy streets or climbing stairs, women could walk and climb freely in this style. Amelia Bloomer, editor of a women's newspaper called *The Lily,* advertised the trousers, and they were promptly dubbed "bloomers."

As a few rebellious souls began wearing the bloomer costume, they were sometimes jeered at, hit with stones, and chased by crowds of boys. Satirical cartoons showed women wearing bloomers and smoking cigars.

Another current fashion was a woman's elaborate hairdo, which took hours to style. Susan B. Anthony decided she had better things to do and cut her hair short. Doing so was a radical gesture of freedom, and few women were willing to endure the criticism it would cause.

Newspapers mocked not only so-called mannish styles but also mannish ideas. In 1852 the *New York Herald* published an editorial that called women's rights activists old maids, ill-mated wives, or mannish women determined to consign man "to his proper sphere—nursing the babies, washing the dishes, mending stockings, and sweeping the house."

The editorial also pointed out the problems that would come if women entered public life. It asked readers to consider "how funny it would sound in the newspapers" to report that a female lecturer in the middle of a speech or a doctor in the middle of an examination

This ad for bloomers ran in an 1851 edition of The Lily, *edited by Amelia Bloomer.*

suddenly had to halt what she was doing—and leave to have a baby. Women were happier at home, the editorial argued. "How did woman first become subject to man as she now is all over the world?" it asked. "By her nature, her sex . . . doomed to subjection; but happier than she would be in any other condition, just because it is the law of her nature."

At a women's rights convention in Cincinnati, Ohio, in 1855, one speaker claimed the movement was based on nothing but the complaints of "a few disappointed women." Speaker Lucy Stone responded

Lucy Stone, **left,** *defied tradition by not taking her husband's last name.*

by saying, yes, she was disappointed. "Disappointment," she said, "is the lot of women." Stone explained that she had watched in frustration and envy as her brothers had attended college and pursued jobs of their choice. God had not blundered by giving women the capacity to do anything, she said. She said she wished ordinary women, "instead of begging of their fathers . . . the latest and gayest new bonnet, would ask of them their rights."

Stone drew attention to women's issues when she married but kept her maiden name, a gesture that was probably equally as startling as Susan B. Anthony's hairstyle. Women who followed her example became known as "Lucy Stoners."

STILL DISAPPOINTED

By 1860 most states allowed married women to own some property. Woman suffrage continued to meet opposition, however. And the cause of abolition grew more pressing every year. In 1863 Stanton and Anthony founded the National Woman's Loyal League, which petitioned Congress to free all slaves.

With the bloody upheaval of the Civil War from 1861 to 1865, most women's rights issues were put aside. After the war, the

Thirteenth Amendment to the U.S. Constitution finally ended slavery. The main goal of the abolition movement had been attained.

However, many rights for African Americans, including voting rights, remained cloudy. Stanton supported universal suffrage—the vote for freed slaves and also for women. But when the Fourteenth Amendment was passed in 1866, making black men eligible to vote, women of all colors and status remained disenfranchised.

Many black women felt they could ill afford to join the fight for women's rights. For them, racism posed a far more immediate threat. At a women's rights convention in 1866, one African American woman, Frances Ellen Watkins Harper, expressed the priorities this way. "You white women speak of rights," she said. "I speak of wrongs." Some sympathizers urged patience; the vote for black men would pave the way for women.

The abolition movement, and to some extent the temperance movement, had taught American women some keen lessons about political organization. In 1868 Stanton and Anthony formed the Working Women's Association to help working women unionize. In 1869 they founded the National Woman Suffrage Association with Stanton as president. That organization had a sharply focused goal: the passage of a constitutional amendment granting women the right to vote.

A handful of women chose to vote without an amendment. Although the Constitution did not say women could vote, it also did not specify that they could not. To force the issue, Susan B. Anthony cast a ballot in 1872 in Rochester, New York. She was promptly arrested. The judge who heard Anthony's case did not allow the jury to reach a verdict. Instead, he pronounced her guilty of the "crime of voting" and fined her one hundred dollars. Anthony responded, "I shall never pay a dollar of your unjust penalty." The incident made front-page news. Outrage about the unfairness of the proceedings inspired more people to support the women's rights movement.

NEVER GIVE IN, NEVER GIVE UP

It was no laughing matter then to break through the customs, prejudices, and established rules . . . but "can't" has ever been unknown to me.
—Bethenia Owens-Adair, Oregon's first female physician, 1874

Between 1840 and 1870, a quarter of a million pioneers traveled westward across the continental United States. For many, the trip offered adventure, the possibility of free land, and a better life. Certainly some women shared this vision, but others saw the trip differently. A long westward journey posed constant dangers to families. Women had heard of youngsters who tumbled out of covered wagons and were run over. River crossings might lead to drownings. Death by diseases such as cholera, typhoid, and mountain fever killed

Abigail Scott Duniway founded a women's rights newspaper called the New Northwest.

pioneers of all ages. More than one in four women who journeyed west were pregnant; many died in childbirth.

Abigail Scott Duniway was one of many women whose experiences influenced her support of the women's rights movement. She had been seventeen when her father took her family from Illinois to Oregon, even though no one else in the family had wanted to go. Her mother and youngest brother died of disease on the Oregon Trail. Abigail married Ben Duniway and had six children. After Ben was disabled, she supported her family by opening a hat shop. A determined woman, she came to live by the slogan "Never give in; never give up."

By 1870 twenty-two years had passed since the Seneca Falls convention. Yet women still did not have the right to vote. The women's rights movement needed people with Duniway's unflagging persistence, who would not let the cause of woman suffrage fade.

In 1871 Duniway began publishing a women's rights newspaper called the *New Northwest*. She wrote and published article after article embracing woman suffrage. She also joined Susan B. Anthony in a lecture tour that year and continued traveling long after, campaigning for suffrage.

Noted for her sharp common sense, Duniway sometimes asked the people in a crowd, "Don't you consider your mother as good, if not better, than an ordinary Salem [Oregon] saloon bum?" One boy who grew up to become governor of Oregon later remembered thinking, "Sure I do." Yet saloon bums could vote, and women could not.

Once on a stagecoach ride, another passenger started to argue with Duniway about women's rights. "Madam," he said, "You ought to be at home, enjoying yourself, like my wife is doing. I want to bear all the hardship of life myself, and let her sit by the fire, toasting her footsies." When that traveler got off the stagecoach at his house, passengers on the coach could see his wife chopping wood for the woodpile. Duniway called out, "I see, my friend, that your wife is toasting her footsies!" His nickname from then on was "Old Footsie Toaster."

Bethenia Owens-Adair, who became Oregon's first female doctor in 1874, often contributed articles to the *New Northwest*. Fewer than 1 percent of the nation's physicians were women at that time. In fact, the author of one medical book wrote that women had heads "almost too small for intellect but just big enough for love." Writing in her autobiography, Owens-Adair said, "I realized early in life that a girl was hampered and hemmed in on all sides, simply by the accident of sex . . . . It was no laughing matter . . . to break through the customs, prejudices, and established rules."

Like Duniway, who was her friend, Owens-Adair possessed a sturdy determination. The word "can't," she declared, "has ever been unknown to me." Her articles in the *New Northwest* and her pioneering example as a female physician both contributed to the cause of women's rights.

Western states—Wyoming, Colorado, and Utah—were the first in the nation to pass laws allowing women to vote in state elections. Despite the efforts of Duniway, Owens-Adair, and others, however, voters in Oregon continued to turn down woman suffrage for many years. And the question of women voting in national elections remained unresolved.

"SMASH, WOMEN, SMASH!"

By the 1870s, the temperance movement had made a significant impact, and many Midwestern states had passed laws controlling the use of alcohol. Even so, few town officials enforced them. Women's efforts to stop the problems caused by liquor reached a high pitch in 1873. Since women had no direct political power, they used prayer vigils, demonstrations, and hymn-sings to make their point.

One morning after a temperance lecture in Hillsboro, Ohio, eighty women met in church. They decided to sing and pray daily in the town's saloons until the owners agreed to close them.

One young Hillsboro man who had just returned home from visiting in Cincinnati, not knowing about the women's plans. He and a few of his friends strolled into a bar and ordered drinks. They were startled to hear the rustle of women's skirts, since only men patronized saloons. They looked up to see what seemed like "a crowd of a thousand ladies entering." One young man spied his mother and sister, another saw two of his cousins, and a third was shocked to see his future mother-in-law in the crowd. The drinkers quickly left.

Carry Nation was one of the most colorful leaders of the liquor protests. She was famous for raising a hatchet and yelling, "Smash, women, smash!" as she led squadrons of women in raids on Kansas saloons in Medicine Lodge and Kiowa. Nation's much-publicized forays became known as "hatchetations." Damaging other people's property was against the law, but Carry Nation ransacked bars that were not licensed or legal. The police did not arrest her for damaging illegal goods.

In the winter of 1873 to 1874, more than sixty thousand women crusaded through the streets of Ohio and Michigan for the "dry" cause. Their numbers—rather than their hatchets—succeeded in closing down more than one thousand saloons.

Middle-class women flocked to join the Women's Christian Temperance Union (WCTU), a pro-family organization that Frances Willard headed beginning in 1874. Through the WCTU, women could work for temperance on a national level apart from men. Newcomers to the temperance movement discovered for the first time their ability to forge social change. They organized not only to restrict alcohol but also to strengthen education for children, to improve conditions for prisoners, and to support other causes. Many young temperance workers ultimately also joined the fight for woman suffrage that had begun more than a quarter of a century earlier.

A photo taken in 1934 shows Carry Nation holding the weapons she used in fighting temperance sixty years earlier—a Bible and a hatchet.

In 1874 temperance crusaders protest the drinking of liquor outside a local saloon.

WHOSE CELEBRATION?

In 1876 the United States marked the centennial of the nation's founding. A gala centennial exposition was to be held in Philadelphia, Pennsylvania. The National Woman Suffrage Association decided to use the celebration to further its own mission. Susan B. Anthony, Elizabeth Cady Stanton, Matilda Joslyn Gage, and others set up a temporary headquarters in a Philadelphia hotel, with Anthony renting the room. (As the only single woman in the group, only she could legally rent it.) By this time, Stanton and Anthony were aged sixty-one and fifty-six; nearly thirty years had passed since the Seneca Falls convention.

Stanton wrote to General Joseph Hawley, the man in charge of the Fourth of July program, requesting "seats for at least one representative woman from each State." When he turned down the request, she responded, "Women will be taxed to pay the expenses of this celebration, and we have as good a right to that platform . . . as the men have, and we will be heard."

When July 4 arrived, a speaker read the 1776 Declaration of Independence to a large crowd in an assembly hall. As he finished, Susan B. Anthony and four officers of the National Woman Suffrage Association walked to the stage and handed him the "Declaration of Sentiments." Amid the uproar that followed, they distributed copies of the declaration to people in the crowd.

Then they marched over to Independence Hall. There Anthony read the declaration to a crowd of waiting supporters. While the centennial exposition marked one hundred years of freedom, women still lacked many freedoms, she said. She concluded, "We ask justice, we ask equality, we ask that all the civil and political rights that belong to citizens of the United States, be guaranteed to us and our daughters forever."

The Philadelphia centennial exposition featured many exhibits (such as one that showed seven kinds of kindergartens) and demonstrations of new inventions. To the thousands of people who visited the exposition, the women's rights leaders also demonstrated once again the exclusion of women from the nation's fundamental rights of citizenship.

WOMEN IN THE LABOR MOVEMENT

The struggle to unionize American workers, begun in the early 1800s, continued through the century. One of the most remarkable leaders in the labor union movement was Mary Harris Jones. An Irish immigrant, she was widowed in 1867 when her husband and their four small children died in a yellow fever epidemic in Memphis, Tennessee. She moved to Chicago and joined the Knights of Labor, which was trying to organize workers to fight for better wages and working conditions. "Mother Jones," as she was nicknamed, devoted the next fifty years of her life to organizing thousands of industrial workers. Because of her effectiveness in leading strikes, one corporate attorney called her "the most dangerous woman in America."

On one occasion, a Pennsylvania miners' strike in 1900, Mother Jones organized miners' wives to picket against scabs—nonunion men who took the jobs of the strikers. On the day the women planned to picket, they assembled armed with mops and brooms. Mother Jones

Mary Harris Jones, known as "Mother" Jones, crisscrossed the nation for fifty years, urging men, women, and child workers to fight for their rights by forming labor unions.

told them, "Be ready to chase the scabs with your mops and brooms. Don't be afraid of anyone." As the "broomstick brigade" marched up to the mine entrance, they waved their "weapons" and beat on tin pans. The *Washington Post* described one woman in the brigade who "started such a racket by beating her dishpan with a hammer and finally throwing the pan at a mule's head that a stampede started." When critics accused Mother Jones of inciting violence, she responded, "The militant, not the meek, shall inherit the earth."

Mother Jones, who could have supported the fight for woman suffrage, had little interest in it. "You don't need a vote to raise hell!" she said. To her, putting food on the table of a miner's family was more important than the vote. "No matter what your fight," she told the women who joined her on the picket lines, "don't be ladylike!"

Women workers still worked for wages lower than men's. To save money, employers sometimes replaced male employees with cheaper female workers. Not surprisingly, many unions opposed working

Charlotte Perkins Gilman, writer and economist, advocated financial independence for women.

In the early 1900s, thousands of textile workers in Passaic, New Jersey, went on strike.

women, believing that women took jobs away from men. A member of the American Federation of Labor declared, "It is wrong to permit any of the female sex of our country to be forced to work, as we believe that the man should be provided with a fair wage in order to keep his female relatives from going to work."

In 1898 Charlotte Perkins Gilman declared this attitude unfair in a landmark book called *Women and Economics.* Gilman believed all women—with jobs or not, rich or poor, married or single—needed economic independence. Standing at the radical edge of the women's rights movement, Gilman predicted the twentieth-century woman would be "a mother economically free; a world-servant instead of a house-servant." Most ordinary people, however, found it difficult to imagine that a woman's place was in the world rather than in the home.

Unionization of women faltered. But a few strikes did succeed. In Lawrence, Massachusetts, women worked the same hours in the mills that their husbands did but earned less pay. The women went on strike, carrying signs that said, "We want bread and roses too." When most of the Lawrence strikers' demands were eventually met, poet James Openheim declared, "The rising of the women means the rising of the race."

HUMAN BIOLOGY

As with generations of women before them, most married women in the 1800s spent their adult lives bearing children. But sex and pregnancy were rarely discussed, especially by women. Even in a woman's private diary, she rarely mentioned her own pregnancies or those of her friends.

Birth control drugs and devices to prevent pregnancies were not readily available in the nineteenth century. In addition, laws, customs, and religious teachings discouraged or forbade birth control methods. The Comstock Law of 1873 designated information about contraception "obscene." Anyone mailing or receiving obscene information could be fined or imprisoned. Because a husband was presumed to have the right to have sex with his wife whenever he wished, women were left with little ability to control the number of children they conceived. Few women, however, connected women's biology to the women's rights movement.

Then along came Victoria Woodhull. Daring and beautiful, she startled many people by her flamboyant attitudes. She divorced her husband and campaigned for suffrage. She even ran for U.S. president in 1872 on the Equal Rights Party ticket.

Even more shocking, Victoria Woodhull declared that women had the right to control their own sexuality. Woodhull said a husband's power over his wife's body reduced her role to "legal prostitution." Married or not, a woman had the right to make her own choices about her own body.

Many women tried to gain control in indirect ways. They complained of "nerves," a vague condition that included headaches, fatigue, anxiety, and boredom. Having nerves was so common that one woman in Milwaukee said, "I do not know one healthy woman in the place." Some middle-class and wealthy women spent weeks at resorts that boasted that their warm water pools could cure women's ills. Away from their husbands, some women may have felt more in charge of their lives.

By the 1890s, American girls were taking physical education classes. They swam, biked, and played golf and tennis. When some women wore bloomers for these activities, they faced far less criticism

In 1899 these girls from Western High School in Washington, D.C., wore bloomers to play basketball. "Proper" girls had more and more freedom for physical activity in the decades that followed.

than had the women of the 1850s. But a woman's freedom to control her own sexuality was still a long way off.

"PLEASE TELL ME THE SECRET"

The fact that most married women bore many children was especially hard on poor women in city slums. Every added baby meant more health problems for the mother, more crowding, less money for doctors, and more poverty for the whole family. These problems led to a high death rate for youngsters. In fact, in the early 1900s, the United States had one of the highest infant mortality rates in the world.

Margaret Higgins Sanger, a public health nurse, gave many speeches describing the plight of poor families burdened with more children than they could provide for. She also told many ordinary people's stories in her book *My Fight for Birth Control.*

The story of Jake and Sadie Sachs was typical. On a hot July day in 1912, Jake, a truck driver, returned to his cramped, New York City slum apartment to find his three children crying and his frail, twenty-eight-year-old wife unconscious. Sadie Sachs had tried to give herself an abortion. She knew her latest pregnancy would add another baby to their family that they could not provide for.

Jake Sachs frantically called a doctor, an expense the family could not afford. The doctor asked Margaret Higgins Sanger to help him. Sanger took care of Sadie Sachs for two weeks until the doctor said, "Her recovery [is] in sight." Sadie Sachs asked the doctor how she could prevent another pregnancy. Instead of giving her a serious answer, he quipped, "Tell Jake to sleep on the roof."

Even if the doctor had had information about contraceptives, he could not have informed Sadie because of the Comstock Law of 1873. "To me it was outrageous," Sanger later said, "that information regarding motherhood, which was so generally called sacred, should be classed with pornography."

Sanger watched Sadie Sachs's face fill with "absolute despair." "We simply looked at each other, saying no word until the door had closed behind the doctor," Sanger wrote. "Then she lifted her thin, blue-veined hands and clasped them beseechingly. 'He can't understand. He's only a man. But you do, don't you? Please tell me the secret . . . . Please!'"

Sanger felt helpless, for she knew no secret way to prevent pregnancy. She also didn't know whether Jake Sachs would "sleep on the roof." A mother of three herself, she did know that most married women had little control over becoming pregnant. Three months later, Margaret Higgens Sanger was called to the Sachs's home again, but there was nothing Sanger could do. Sadie Sachs, pregnant again, had died.

PLAIN FACTS

Like Victoria Woodhull a generation earlier, Sanger believed a woman should be "absolute mistress of her own body." She wanted all women to have the choice of "voluntary motherhood." The plight of women like Sadie Sachs propelled Sanger to devote her life to learning more about birth control and then teaching others—even though society disapproved of these activities.

In 1912 Sanger wrote a series of articles on "What Every Girl Should Know" for a radical newspaper named *The Call.* Because one article talked about sexually transmitted disease, it was declared obscene. That issue of *The Call* was confiscated by the U.S. postal service. In response, *The Call* printed an issue that repeated the headline "What Every Girl Should Know." It was followed by an abruptly short statement: "NOTHING, by order of the Post-Office Department."

Intent on learning more about contraceptives, Sanger traveled to Europe, where birth control information was more available. When she returned to the United States, she started a newsletter, *The Woman Rebel.* In 1914 she introduced the term "birth control." When *The Woman Rebel* said women should be free to get information about birth control, it was quickly barred from the mail.

Margaret Higgens Sanger, **right,** *researched trends in pregnancy. She eventually founded Planned Parenthood to help women plan their families.*

On October 16, 1916, Sanger opened a two-room birth control clinic in a poor Brooklyn neighborhood mostly inhabited by Jewish and Italian immigrants. To publicize the clinic, she and two colleagues distributed fliers printed in English, Yiddish, and Italian. The fliers said:

> Mothers!
> Can you afford to have a large family?
> Do you want any more children?
> If not, why do you have them?
> Do not kill, do not take life, but prevent....

Women lined up outside the clinic and waited from dawn to dusk to receive the information Sanger was handing out about birth control. In slightly over a week, Sanger "talked plain talk and gave plain facts" to about five hundred women.

As it turned out, one "patient" was a police officer in disguise. A few days after the officer's visit, police raided the clinic. They arrested Sanger and jailed her for a short time, but the ensuing publicity rallied support for her cause.

Nonetheless, sex and pregnancy remained mostly taboo topics. Many people continued to oppose the use of birth control and abortions, often on religious grounds.

AT LAST

When Woodrow Wilson arrived in Washington, D.C., on March 3, 1913, to take office as the country's new president, few people welcomed him. Women's rights activist Alice Paul, head of the National Woman's Party (NWP), had scheduled a suffrage parade to match the date of his arrival. Instead of greeting Wilson, a crowd of half a million watched eight thousand people march to demand the vote for women.

Some spectators strongly opposed woman suffrage. When some of them began to get out of hand, Genevieve Stone, wife of a congressman, asked a policeman to help protect the marchers. He refused. "If my wife were where you are, I'd break her head," he said. Two hundred suffragists were injured.

Alice Paul's parade was one of many suffrage rallies that took place all around the nation. The National American Woman Suffrage Association (NAWSA) was also lobbying hard for the vote. (It had been formed when the National Woman Suffrage Association merged with another group.) Even so, Congress did not grant woman suffrage, and groups like the National Anti-Suffrage Association opposed it. In the early twentieth century, a woman's role was still thought to be in the home.

Then in 1917, the United States entered World War I. The U.S. army ballooned from two hundred thousand to four million soldiers. With so many men away fighting, the country urgently needed people to replace them in the workforce. Many women quickly took jobs in factories, producing goods for the war effort. By 1918 eight million women were employed.

World War I ended in 1918. President Woodrow Wilson wrote to the president of the NAWSA, Carrie Chapman Catt. "The services of women during the supreme crisis have been of the most signal usefulness . . . ," Wilson said. "It is high time that part of our debt should be acknowledged and paid."

The next year, Congress passed the Nineteenth Amendment to the U.S. Constitution. If ratified by at least thirty-six states, it would give American women the right to vote. At the same time, the Eighteenth Amendment was circulating for ratification. When it passed and took effect in January 1920, it banned the sale of liquor, and the long-sought goal of temperance was won.

On March 3, 1913, women in Washington, D.C., and in many other cities marched for the right to vote. Here suffragists in New York City join the cause.

In September 1920, a woman hands over her ballot in the first election open to all American women.

Then in August 1920, Tennessee became the last state needed for ratification of the woman suffrage amendment. The "most momentous reform" finally became law—seventy-two years after Elizabeth Cady Stanton had first proposed it in Seneca Falls. For twenty-six million newly enfranchised women, not giving in and not giving up had paid off after all.

FROM APRONS TO OVERALLS—AND BACK

The ballot is the symbol of a new status in human society, it is the greatest possible single step forward in the progress of women, but it does not in itself complete their freedom.
      —The *Suffragist,* 1920

During the "Roaring Twenties," many young women became "flappers." Flappers bobbed their hair short, listened to jazz, and danced the night away. A flapper was supposed to be thin, not generously sized as women had been.

In this more liberated age, the topic of sex became less taboo. Women bared their legs, wearing skirts with hemlines above the knees. They went swimming in brief tank suits. Some women found ways to buy contraceptives, even though contraceptives were still illegal.

When American soldiers returned to work after World War I, most middle-class women left their wartime jobs and went home. In Elizabeth Cady Stanton's day, the "true" woman had hired servants to do the housework. By the 1920s, electricity was bringing new labor-saving devices into the American home, and a woman proudly did her own housework. As an editorial in the *Ladies Home Journal* in February 1928 put it, "The fact is that the American home was never a more satisfying place than it is today. Science and invention have outfitted it with a great range of conveniences and comforts . . . . All this is, in the main, women's work."

Besides, hired help was expensive. Researchers Robert S. Lynd and Helen M. Lynd did a study in Muncie, Indiana, that showed costs for domestic help had risen sharply. In 1924 a housewife in Muncie paid as much for a single day's work by a domestic as her mother had spent for a week's labor.

Even more than keeping house, women were expected to be good mothers. Wealthy women in the 1800s had hired nursemaids to care for their children. In the 1920s, a mother was viewed as shortchanging her offspring if she handed them over to a servant. Only a mother could give a child the love, care, and attention needed. "I accommodate my entire life to my little girl," one Muncie, Indiana, woman told the Lynds.

After the Miss America Beauty Pageant began in 1921, Miss America came to personify the ideal woman. Samuel Gompers of the

Flappers show off their legs during a dance contest in January 1926.

American Federation of Labor described the first Miss America to the *New York Times*. "She represents the type of womanhood America needs," he said, "strong, red-blooded, able to shoulder the responsibilities of home-making and motherhood. It is in her type that the hope of the country resides."

As for "working girls" in the booming economy of the 1920s, even female college graduates held mostly low-paying jobs. "Feminine" job titles included nurse, secretary, salesgirl, bookkeeper, and maid. Carrie Chapman Catt said she looked forward to the day when a woman "as well qualified as a man to fill a position . . . shall have an equal and unprejudiced chance to secure it."

By this time, women's groups such as the National Women's Trade Union League had won many maximum-hour laws, minimum-wage laws, and other laws intended to protect women in the workplace. Protective legislation gave women special consideration (for example, maximum-hour laws ordered that employers must allow women to leave work earlier than men each day).

EQUAL RIGHTS, YET NOT

After so many decades of fighting for the vote, women's rights advocates faced a crisis in the 1920s. The vote had been won. What should the next step be?

Women were treated inequitably under thousands of state laws covering divorce rights, property rights, work opportunities, and other issues. As Alice Paul of the National Woman's Party put it in 1921, "Women today . . . are still in every way subordinate to men before the law, in the professions, in the church, in industry, and in the home."

The League of Women Voters (LWV) had become the nation's leading women's rights group. The LWV and similar organizations believed that needed reforms would be won gradually through the vote. The more radical, smaller NWP (it had just eight thousand members) said the vote was not enough.

In 1923 the NWP proposed an Equal Rights Amendment (ERA) to the U.S. Constitution. Designed to eliminate discriminatory laws in one fell swoop, the proposed amendment declared, "Men and women shall have equal rights throughout the United States and every place subject to its jurisdiction."

The LWV opposed the ERA, since it would alienate many people. "The LWV...has stood for step by step progress...," declared its first president. "It has not sought to lead a few women a long way quickly, but rather to lead many women a little way at a time."

In addition, the LWV believed the ERA threatened protective legislation, which might be struck down as unconstitutional if the proposed amendment passed. Thus, while the ERA might eliminate some bad laws, it would sweep away many good ones. "The Equal Rights Amendment would operate like a blind man with a shot gun," advised one lawyer. "No [one] can confidently predict what it would hit."

The NWP responded that protective legislation didn't really protect women anyway. For example, Harvard University in Cambridge, Massachusetts, fired twenty scrubwomen when the state ordered their wages increased by two cents an hour. Another example was Molly Maloney, a bookbinder in New York City. She had worked the night shift until 1919, when New York passed a law saying women could not work after 10 P.M. To work days, Maloney had to take a cut in pay. Then New York declared women could not work overtime. When Maloney couldn't keep up with rush orders within a normal workday, she lost her job. "We working women can protect ourselves," she declared, as if asking New York to stop helping her, "if we have equality of opportunity under the law."

The debate over the ERA grew heated at times. The women's rights movement had lost its strongest leaders (Elizabeth Cady Stanton had died in 1902; Susan B. Anthony in 1906). Alice Paul was leading the NWP in tactics many questioned (such as burning President Wilson in effigy). And no strong new leaders stepped forward to help unify everyone. Lacking the support of the whole women's movement, and with no compromise in sight, the ERA stalled indefinitely.

THE CRASH

During the Great Depression of the 1930s, the U.S. economy crashed, leaving thousands of people bankrupt and jobless. As many as one man in four found himself unemployed.

Almost always, women who worked "had" to work. The money was needed because a family did not have a husband and father, or he was ill or unemployed. Even so, many people saw women's wages as "pin money"—money to be spent on little extras. In 1936, one of the first public opinion polls by George Gallup showed that four out of five Americans felt any available jobs should go to men instead of married women, who presumably had a man to support them.

Newlyweds Lillie Gleason and Dean Maddux of Omaha, Nebraska, kept their marriage a secret. Lillie's union had a policy that said, "Married women whose husbands have permanent positions . . . should be discriminated against in the hiring of employees." Lillie feared that if her boss found out she had gotten married, she might be fired from her job as a bookkeeper. She and Dean needed her income to help support Lillie's mother and Dean's younger brother and sister.

Managing a household on a tightened budget wasn't easy, so the depression increased people's respect for many household skills. To save money, women learned how to fix electric motors and paint used furniture. They sewed curtains and mended clothes, much as earlier generations of women had done. Women's magazines handed out tips on careful shopping.

Eleanor Roosevelt, who became the nation's First Lady when her husband Franklin Delano Roosevelt was elected president in 1932, encouraged women to get involved in politics. "Get into the game and stay in it," she advised. "Throwing mud from the outside won't help. Building up from the inside will." She became the first president's wife to hold a press conference. She traveled around the nation as her husband's "eyes and ears," talking to people to find out what they needed, then lobbying on their behalf back in Washington, D.C.

Perhaps one of the most significant changes for women came in 1937. That year, doctors in the United States won the legal right to dispense birth control information. In 1942 Margaret Higgens Sanger named her organization Planned Parenthood.

Many people still opposed contraception, however. For example, the Catholic Church forbade its members to use contraceptives. Every year, thousands of women had unwanted pregnancies. And thousands got illegal abortions to end them.

As for the ban on alcohol, it had been lifted in late 1933. Prohibition had led to more problems than it had solved, as gangsters took up an illegal traffic in booze. The cause of temperance faded away.

SINCE YOU WENT AWAY

On December 7, 1941, the Japanese bombed a U.S. military base at Pearl Harbor in Hawaii. Once again, life changed for American men and women. The United States swiftly entered World War II, and the phrase "home front" took on a new meaning.

During the war, women were asked to leave their places at home and enter the workforce. Patriotic posters featured "Rosie the Riveter," a symbol of the women needed to fill "men's jobs." "We Can Do It!" Rosie told American women as she flexed a muscular arm.

In other propaganda, the U.S. government encouraged women not to shy away from men's work by making analogies to chores familiar to women. Help wanted ads compared an industrial crane to "a gigantic clothes wringer" and a steel-cutting machine to a large pair of "scissors." The job of winding wire spools was much like "crocheting."

Soon "cleaning ladies," clerical workers, and teachers were quitting their jobs and working for better wages in factories. Housewives gave blood, economized on goods needed by the military, and took on the chores of their absent husbands. In one popular movie, *Since You Went Away*, a mother made the "sacrifice" of getting a job as a welder while her husband was at war.

Nova Lee McGhee Holbrook was a real-life woman who worked as a welder during the war. Her boss at the Kaiser Shipyard in Richmond, California, warned her that welding "was going to be dirty." Telling the story years later, she remembered answering, "I can wash it off."

The United States played a big role in feeding the Allies during the war. With many farmers away fighting, women pitched in to help plant and harvest crops. Some farm managers resisted hiring women to do hot, dirty work and handle massive farm equipment. Part of the mission of the U.S. Crop Corps, established by the federal government in 1943, was to show that women could handle farmwork.

Many women discovered they liked their new work environment. Mary Entwistle Poole of Tiburon, California, left her low-paying

Women eagerly stepped up to take over the many "male" jobs left open when men went to war during World War II. These women worked in a shipyard in 1942.

teaching job during the war. Like Nova Holbrook, she also worked as a welder and liked earning "men's wages." "The only reason welding was a man's job," she discovered, "is that men had always done it." Interviewed long after thewar, she said that job "gave me a good start in life . . . . I decided if I could learn to weld like a man, I could do anything it took to make a living."

STARTING A BABY BOOM

World War II ended in 1945. When the soldiers returned, most women were forced out of their wartime jobs. Jennie Fain Folan and her four children had left their Arkansas farm and moved to Tacoma, Washington, in 1942. She had found a job building ships.

The day the war was over, "We were all laid off," she said. "The union didn't stand for us because we were women." To support herself and the children, Folan began working in a hotel where she earned far less than the shipyard had paid her.

Some women who had been domestics before the war lost their better-paying factory jobs and had to clean houses again. Many of these women were African American. In the 1950s, Beatrice Thornton, a black woman, left her small, rented house in Rochester, New York, every morning to ride a bus out to an affluent suburb with white residents. When the bus doors opened, Thornton and a dozen other African American "cleaning ladies" stepped out, each carrying a paper bag containing her work clothes for the day. At dusk, they returned to their own segregated neighborhoods.

Many other female factory workers, truck drivers, and shipbuilders who shed their work uniforms moved into houses in the suburbs. Middle-class men boasted, "No wife of mine will ever have to work." Advertisers agreed. According to them, new consumer products such as frozen foods and automatic appliances made housekeeping easier than ever. Their products helped housewives in frilly aprons and high heels solve every problem from "ring around the collar" to "waxy buildup" on linoleum floors. Postwar couples in these efficient homes

Many praised women's wartime work but still believed that women should not remain in the labor force. In the first year after World War II, 3.25 million women lost their jobs. This ad promotes the Hoover brand of vacuums, but it also reflects the underlying notion that women would be happier at home.

had so many offspring that their children were dubbed "baby boomers."

Although the "typical" American woman seemed to spend her time banishing ring around the collar, not every woman followed this pattern. About one-third of the nation's mothers worked outside the home. More than half of the new female employees did low-paying clerical work. Women also worked as teachers, nurses, librarians, sales clerks, and domestics. As one woman, Miyako Moriki, recalled, the middle-class Japanese American women she had known during this era "went into nursing and teaching, and all the men went into engineering, technical fields." On average, women earned slightly more than half of what men earned.

MAKE COFFEE, NOT POLICY

The fight for women's rights and civil rights for African Americans intersected once again in the 1950s. At that time, many African

Americans in the North lived, like Beatrice Thornton, in neighborhoods that "happened" to be mostly black. Segregation in the South was less subtle. Many southern states had laws requiring whites and African Americans to attend separate schools, drink from separate drinking fountains, and sit in separate sections of buses and trains. The U.S. Supreme Court had ruled these laws to be constitutional as long as the separate facilities were equal.

Then in 1955, in Montgomery, Alabama, the driver of an overcrowded bus ordered Rosa Parks to give up her seat to a white man who was standing. Parks refused, and she was jailed and fined. A tumultuous protest led by Dr. Martin Luther King Jr. followed. It ended with a Supreme Court ruling in 1956 that declared segregated seating on public buses to be unconstitutional. Separate—by its very nature, as the justices ruled in this case and others—could not be equal.

But the fight for civil rights had just begun. Through the late 1950s and into the 1960s, women and men, black and white, joined protest marches all around the nation, demanding changes both in laws and in customs.

As the civil rights movement progressed, however, many women found themselves limited to menial tasks such as folding fliers. They were expected, as some reported, to "make coffee, not policy." The attitude underlying this experience, according to civil rights activists Casey Hayden and Mary King, was "as deep-rooted and every much as crippling to the woman as the assumptions of white superiority are to the Negro."

Thus women found their roles—whether at home, in the workplace, or in the civil rights movement—to be separate from men's. Without a strong women's movement leading the way, those separate roles seemed destined to remain unequal.

SISTERHOOD IS POWERFUL

We don't just want a bigger piece of the pie. We want to change the recipe.

— 1970s feminist slogan on buttons and T-shirts

In the early 1960s, Congress debated a civil rights bill in which race and gender were again linked. The bill forbade discrimination in employment on account of race. Then a congressman added a section called Title VII to the bill forbidding discrimination on account of gender. Supporters of Title VII hoped it would help women blast through the "glass ceiling"—the invisible place near the top of a company hierarchy that a woman could not rise above. In 1964 the Civil Rights Act became law, and President Lyndon Johnson set up the Equal Employment Opportunity Commission (EEOC) to enforce it.

Popular acceptance of the new law was another matter. Many people thought that treating men and women differently sometimes just made sense. The personnel officer of a large airline company wondered what to do "when a gal walks into our office, demands a job as an airline pilot, and has the credentials to qualify." To him, hiring a woman to fly a huge aircraft was unthinkable.

Some cartoons and editorials made the same point in a more exaggerated way. An editorial in the *New York Times* in 1965 wondered what would happen if a man wanted to be a bunny at a Playboy Club, where waitresses wore scanty bunny costumes. Would Playboy have to hire him? Title VII was soon sarcastically dubbed the "bunny law."

Even the EEOC seemed slow to accept Title VII. For example, it approved newspaper ads that listed separate jobs for males and females. It booked a meeting at a private club that excluded women. Finally one member of the EEOC, Aileen Clarke Hernandez, resigned, saying the EEOC itself was discriminatory.

NOW, NOT LATER

When speaking of the chance of winning suffrage, Susan B. Anthony had said, "Failure is impossible." The first, long wave of the women's rights movement that had begun in the 1850s did bring women the vote in 1920. The 1960s brought a second wave of feminist activism that had, by this time, lain dormant for nearly forty years. One of the main inspirations for this second wave came from freelance journalist Betty Friedan.

Friedan had been one of many women who had married after World War II and begun raising a family. She was appalled at the roadblocks women faced in trying to develop their talents. In 1963 she wrote a book called *The Feminine Mystique.* "The core of the problem of women today," she wrote, "is not sexual but a problem of identity—a stunting or evasion of growth."

Friedan described many well-educated, middle-class women who seemed to have everything: a family, a house in the suburbs, a car in the garage. Yet they wanted something . . . more. One reader wrote to Friedan, "In seeking that something 'more' out of life, I have tried large doses of everything from alcohol to religion." Friedan dubbed the vague dissatisfaction that many women felt "the problem that has no name."

In an article called "The Paradox of Progress," historian William H. Chafe commented, "Although Friedan's assessment contained little that had not been said before . . . , her book spoke to millions of women in a fresh way, driving home the message that what had previously been perceived as only a personal problem was in fact a woman problem." *The Feminine Mystique* touched such a nerve with so many people that it not only became a national best-seller but also sparked a nationwide call for change. The "women's liberation movement" was on.

In 1966 Friedan founded the National Organization for Women (NOW). NOW's goal was to "bring women into full participation in the mainstream of American society now." The organization sought both economic change and legal reforms such as enforcement of Title VII. With NOW's encouragement, thousands of women filed complaints under Title VII.

*In the 1960s, Betty Friedan, **right**, of the National Organization for Women prompted a second wave of feminism that led to many legal reforms.*

Members of NOW picket the White House to lobby for the Equal Rights Amendment and other issues taken up by the women's movement in the 1970s.

While women lobbied at the national level, they also met at the grassroots level. Many formed small consciousness-raising groups. Meeting weekly around someone's kitchen table, women in "C.R. groups" described their lives and feelings. They tried to work as partners for change rather than as competitors for men. One woman was relieved to discover in her C.R. group that she was "not the only one struggling to overcome dependency on men."

By 1970 the women's liberation movement had brought women's issues to the top of the public agenda. The Equal Rights Amendment was introduced in Congress again in 1972 and sent to the states for ratification. Twenty-eight states approved it; just ten more were needed. Gloria Steinem began her feminist magazine, *Ms.*, that same year and sold out the first three hundred thousand copies in eight days.

By passing Title IX of the Education Amendments of 1972, Congress denied schools federal financial support unless schools provided equal funding for women's and men's sports. As schools gradually adjusted, girls' lives changed. For example, Sharon Paley, a teenager in Westchester, New York, was athletically inclined and loved sports. But she attended high school before Title IX took effect. As she recalled years later, "I was not encouraged to participate in school sports at all. In fact, only two were available for girls—tennis and track—and little was said about them." In contrast, under Title IX, Sharon Paley's daughters competed in the 1990s on girls' soccer, volleyball, basketball, tennis, and track teams.

HARD TO PRONOUNCE

Even as support for women's liberation grew, so did resistance. Women's rights activists called themselves "feminists," but many newspapers and magazines referred to "women's libbers." A student told one teacher in San Jose, California, that he couldn't call her "Ms." because "I can't pronounce it."

Another mocking label was "bra burners." It began in 1968, when Robin Morgan, Kathie Sarachild, Carol Hanisch, and Alix Kates Schulman, among others, drew national publicity at the Miss America Pageant in Atlantic City, New Jersey. Instead of cheering for Miss America, they crowned their own candidate—a sheep. They also filled a trash can with "instruments of torture to women": high-heeled shoes, bras, girdles, and magazines such as *Playboy*. No record exists of a bra being burned. But after newspapers and magazines used the term "bra burners" to describe the Atlantic City group, the name clung to anyone with feminist ideas.

Phyllis Schlafly, a Harvard-educated lawyer, became the most outspoken opponent of the women's liberation movement. She traveled around the nation, speaking for a conservative coalition called the New Right. In her "Phyllis Schlafly Report," she linked the ERA, *Ms.* magazine, and feminists as "anti-family, anti-children, and pro-abortion."

Phyllis Schlafly addresses a rally of ERA protestors in Alton, Illinois.

Their ideas were "a series of sharptongued, high-pitched, whining complaints by unmarried women." In short, she said, "Women's lib is a total assault on the role of the American woman as wife and mother, and on the family as the basic unit of society."

Schlafly launched a "Stop ERA" campaign and prompted a nationwide debate. The ratification process stalled. Congress then set a deadline of 1982. When time ran out, only thirty-five states had approved the ERA, and once again, it died.

After the defeat of the ERA, Betty Friedan founded the National Women's Political Caucus. Its goal was "to get women into the office." In 1968 Shirley Chisholm had been the first African American

Those who demanded the right to legal abortions became known as "pro-choice" advocates. Here, from left to right, celebrities Morgan Fairchild, Glenn Close, and Jane Fonda join in a pro-choice rally.

woman elected to the House of Representatives. But women in Congress were rare. Friedan hoped to get a more fair proportion of women elected to "make policy, not coffee."

ROE v. WADE

Probably the most bitter debate about women's rights focused on abortion. Feminists echoed Victoria Woodhull and Margaret Sanger by asking, Who has the right to control a woman's body? The birth control pill, first introduced in 1961, made contraception easier and more reliable than in previous generations. Yet unexpected or unwanted pregnancies still occurred.

In 1973 the Supreme Court heard an abortion rights case titled *Roe v. Wade.* The court ruled that antiabortion laws were unconstitutional because they invaded a woman's right to privacy. After that, a woman could choose to have a legal abortion early in her pregnancy.

The *Roe v. Wade* decision did little to stop debate. Antiabortion activists continued to fight for the "right to life." At abortion clinics, medical staff and patients sometimes faced protesters and occasionally violence.

AND ONWARD

A few women did ascend to leadership. In 1984 Democrat Geraldine Ferraro ran for vice president, the first woman to run on the presidential ticket for a major party. The following year, Wilma Mankiller, a member of the Cherokee, became the first woman to lead a major tribal nation. The proportion of women in Congress remained a scanty 5 percent. But in 1996, President Bill Clinton appointed Madeleine Albright as secretary of state, handing the most powerful position in the cabinet to a woman.

Wilma Mankiller, **left,** *first female head of a tribal nation, and Secretary of State Madeleine Albright,* **right,** *reached positions of political authority in the 1980s and 1990s, respectively.*

All through the 1990s, everyday life for women changed in many small ways. Forms routinely offered "Ms." as an option for a woman's title. Labels for many jobs became gender neutral, with terms such as "mailman" changing to "mail carrier." Books, newspapers, and magazines strove for nonsexist grammar. Instead of "a workman needs to get to his job on time," the language became "workers must get to their jobs on time."

Magazines, movies, billboards, and popular television sent out a steady barrage of images about girls. Their ideal girl used expensive makeup, wore stylish clothes, and was painfully thin. In a 1991 book called *The Beauty Myth,* author Naomi Wolf declared, "American women . . . would rather lose ten to fifteen pounds than achieve any other goal." In a best-selling book called *Reviving Ophelia: Saving the Selves of Adolescent Girls,* psychologist Mary Pipher wrote that, just as women of the 1960s struggled with "the problem that has no name," adolescent girls of the 1990s also faced "a problem with no name." Pipher called the United States "a girl-poisoning culture."

Combating this trend, fifty thousand women gathered in Beijing, China, in 1995 at the United Nations Fourth International Conference on Women. They issued statements on violence against women, education of girls and women, health care, and access to financial resources. At the conference, First Lady Hillary Rodham Clinton defined women's rights as "human rights." She included the right to child care, equal employment, and freedom from violence.

As the new millennium opened, it was easy to take the gains of the women's movement for granted. Many young women did not consider themselves "feminists." Whether a woman identified herself as a feminist or not, the women's movement had revolutionized opportunities for women. In 1999 there were more than eight million women-owned businesses in the United States employing twenty-four million people and generating $3.1 trillion dollars in revenue.

Reform in the workplace continued. In 1999 NOW urged the nation's top five hundred employers to voluntarily promise to provide a

In 1995 women from around the world gathered to discuss issues at the United Nations Fourth International Conference on Women in Beijing, China.

workplace free of discrimination based on sex, race, sexual orientation, age, marital status, pregnancy, parenthood, disability, or size. In the year 2000, for the first time since the 1970s, Congress held hearings on the male-female pay gap. It found that women earned on average 76.5 percent of what men made, an improvement from 62.5 percent in 1979.

Roles and rights for women will doubtless continue to evolve. In the 1800s, Elizabeth Cady Stanton had said, "The true woman is as yet a dream of the future." Americans one and all will be shaped by both the failings and strengths of those who came before. As Gloria Steinem put it in an essay entitled "Helping Ourselves to Revolution," "The future depends entirely on what each of us does every day." What each of us does will ultimately reveal whether failure is impossible in the struggle for full equality for American women.

REMARKABLE WOMEN

Many women in addition to those discussed in this book and noted on the timeline on pages 90 and 91 contributed to the progress of women in the United States. Some worked actively for women's rights. Others led lives of distinction, serving as role models for generations that followed. Below are just a few of these women of note. To learn about others, visit the National Women's Hall of Fame website at <http://www.greatwomen.org/index.html>.

MARIAN ANDERSON *(1897–1993)*
A gifted contralto, Anderson was barred from singing at Constitution Hall in Washington, D.C., because she was African American. Thousands showed up to hear her when she performed at the Lincoln Memorial instead. Anderson's achievements made music one of the first arenas in which black Americans enjoyed full acknowledgment.

MAYA ANGELOU *(1923–)*
Angelou overcame childhood poverty and sexual abuse to achieve renown as a poet, novelist, dancer, playwright, and actor. She recited her poem "On the Pulse of Morning" at the 1993 inauguration of President William Clinton. She was the first poet so honored since Robert Frost in 1961.

PRUDENCE CRANDALL *(1803–1890)*
Crandall opened a boarding school for African American girls in Connecticut in 1832. When Connecticut declared it illegal to "instruct colored persons who are not inhabitants of the state," Crandall appealed to the U.S. Supreme Court, which struck down the Connecticut law. Vigilantes harassed Crandall and her students anyway, and Crandall was forced to close her school. Fifty years later, Connecticut officially apologized.

MARY BARRET DYER *(birthdate unknown–1660)*
Like Anne Hutchinson, Dyer defied Puritan authorities in Massachusetts Bay Colony. Before being executed for her Quaker beliefs, Dyer said, "My life not availeth me in comparison to the liberty of truth."

DOLORES HUERTA *(1930–)*
In 1962 Huerta and Cesar Chavez cofounded the United Farm Workers, a union for migrant workers and others. Unemployment insurance, collective bargaining rights, and immigration rights have been just a few of the causes Huerta has championed.

HELEN KELLER *(1880–1968)*

Keller became deaf and blind when she was just nineteen months old. She overcame these handicaps and became a national spokesperson for people with disabilities.

FLORENCE KELLEY *(1859–1932)*

As general secretary of the National Consumers League from 1899 until 1932, Kelley helped bring about minimum wage laws, limited work hours for women, and better working conditions for women and children. In 1912, partly at her urging, Congress established the Federal Children's Bureau.

BILLIE JEAN KING *(1943–)*

A premier tennis player, King won more than twenty Wimbledon titles and thirteen U.S. Open titles. Her 1973 victory in a match against self-described "male chauvinist pig" Bobby Riggs drew a television audience estimated at sixty million viewers worldwide. That same year, she won her long battle for equal prize money and treatment for women professionals in major tennis tournaments.

BELVA LOCKWOOD *(1830–1917)*

Denied permission to argue a case before the U.S. Supreme Court, Lockwood lobbied for laws allowing female lawyers to practice before the court. In 1879 she became the first woman in the nation to do so. Lockwood championed many human rights causes and ran for president in 1884 on the Equal Rights Party ticket.

MARIA GOEPPERT MAYER *(1906–1972)*

Mayer was the first American woman to win the Nobel Prize in physics (1963) and the second woman ever to do so. She began her prize-winning work in developing the shell model of the nucleus of the atom at the Argonne National Laboratory in Chicago, Illinois.

SANDRA DAY O'CONNOR *(1930–)*

After earning a law degree from Stanford University when she was only twenty-two, O'Connor discovered that California law firms would not hire her because she was female. She entered public service instead. She became an Arizona assistant attorney general in 1965, a state senator in 1969, and a superior court judge in 1978. In 1981 she became the first woman appointed to the U.S. Supreme Court.

GEORGIA O'KEEFFE *(1887–1986)*

One of the most original and productive American painters, O'Keeffe developed her own style characterized by stark images of the southwestern desert. She said, "The painting is like a thread that runs through all the reasons for all other things that make one's life."

VINNIE REAM *(1847–1914)*

Born in a log cabin in Madison, Wisconsin, Ream became famous when she won a highly competitive federal commission in the 1870s to sculpt President Abraham Lincoln and Civil War hero Admiral David Farragut. When Ream married in 1878, however, her husband told her, "Now you must live, not for the world, but for love and me." Ream went into retirement for the next twenty-two years.

SALLY RIDE *(1951–)*

In 1983 Ride served as an astronaut and flight engineer aboard the Challenger shuttle, becoming the first American woman to go into space. She completed a second space mission in 1984, logging a total of 337 hours in space.

ANNE ROYALL *(1769–1854)*

In 1831 Royall began publishing a newspaper, the *Paul Pry* (later called *The Huntress),* in Washington, D.C. Roaming the halls of Congress to get her stories, she relentlessly critiqued American life and government. President John Quincy Adams refused to give her an interview. She discovered him swimming one day and sat on his clothes until he agreed to talk with her. She interviewed seven presidents in all.

HARRIET TUBMAN *(c. 1820–1913)*

A former slave, Tubman became known as "the Moses of her people." She led more than three hundred escaping slaves to freedom. As a scout for the Union army during the Civil War (1861–1865), she collected military information and tended wounded soldiers. In 1892 Congress finally granted Tubman a pension for her dangerous wartime work.

WEETAMOO *(birthdate unknown–1676)*

When this Native American leader failed in negotiations to find peaceful solutions to clashes with nearby Puritan settlers, she led more than three hundred warriors into a series of battles against them. Within a year, several settlers noted in letters that Weetamoo and her troops had been destroyed.

IDA B. WELLS-BARNETT *(1862–1931)*

Angered by the murder of three black businessmen in Memphis, Tennessee, journalist and social reformer Wells-Barnett initiated a nationwide campaign in 1891 against lynching—the execution of a person by an angry mob. She wrote many newspaper articles that brought the problem of lynching to the forefront of national attention.

OPRAH WINFREY *(1954–)*

One of the most recognized media personalities in the United States throughout the 1990s, Winfrey is the creator of and host of the *Oprah Winfrey* talk show. She uses the series as a forum for the discussion of varied social problems such as child abuse and human rights, and her book club has prompted millions of daytime viewers to read and discuss literature.

SARAH WINNEMUCCA *(c. 1842–1891)*

A Paiute, Winnemucca served as a peacemaker among hostile western tribes as well as with the U.S. military. Nicknamed "the princess" by whites, she made a lecture tour in the eastern states, selling her *Life Among the Paiutes: Their Wrongs and Claims* and arousing public sympathy for them. The government responded by promising to return land to Native American tribes, but the orders were never carried out.

FRANCES WRIGHT *(1795–1852)*

Wright was one of the first American women to speak publicly against slavery and for equal rights for women. Writing in the *Free Enquirer,* she advocated birth control, more flexible divorce laws, and the reduction of the church's influence in politics. Susan B. Anthony and Elizabeth Cady Stanton considered Wright a mentor.

CHIEN-SHIUNG WU *(1912–1997)*

A naturalized American citizen, Wu was a research scientist whose experiments at Columbia University advanced the understanding of subatomic particles and the fundamental laws governing the physical universe.

MILDRED "BABE" DIDRIKSON ZAHARIAS *(1914–1956)*

Determined to be "the greatest athlete that ever lived," Zaharias won Olympic gold medals in track and field in 1932. She also excelled in baseball, basketball, tennis, boxing, diving, and skating. She had a highly successful twenty-year career as a golfer, and she was a founding member of the Ladies Professional Golf Association.

TIMELINE

ca. 1607 According to legend, Pocahontas saves Captain John Smith from execution

1650 *The Tenth Muse Lately Sprung Up in America* by Anne Bradstreet published, first book of poetry written in North America in English

1692 Salem witch trials

1700

1773 Phillis Wheatley's poetry published in England, the first book written in the colonies by an African American

1775–83 American Revolution

1775

1792 Mary Wollstonecraft, an English woman, publishes *A Vindication of the Rights of Woman*

1804–05 Sacagawea guides Lewis and Clark expedition

1800

1821 First U.S. institution of higher education for girls, Troy Female Seminary, founded

1825

1837 First U.S. women's college, Mount Holyoke Seminary, founded in South Hadley, Massachussetts

1847 Lowell Female Industrial Reform and Mutual Aid Society, one of the earliest women's labor groups, founded

1848 First women's rights convention in Seneca Falls, New York

1849 First woman graduate of a U.S. medical school, Elizabeth Blackwell

1850

1851 Sojourner Truth's "Ain't I a Woman?" speech; bloomers appear

1853 First U.S. female minister, Antoinette Brown, appointed

1861–65 American Civil War

1865 First Congressional Medal of Honor given to a woman, Mary Edwards Walker, a Union surgeon during the Civil War

1866 American Equal Rights Association founded; first YWCA

1875

1900

1925

1950

1975

2000

1869   National Woman Suffrage Association founded; Territory of Wyoming grants women the vote

1876   Elizabeth Cady Stanton, Susan B. Anthony, and Matilda Joslyn Gage write the "Declaration of Sentiments"

ca. 1880s   The typewriter draws women to office work in record numbers

1889–90   Reporter Nellie Bly travels around the world in seventy-two days

1892   Women's basketball begins at Smith College in Northampton, Massachussetts

1895   National Federation of Afro-American Women founded

1914–18   World War I

1916   First woman elected to Congress, Jeannette Pickering Rankin; first American birth control clinic founded by Margaret Sanger

1920   Nineteenth Amendment grants women suffrage

1921   First woman Pulitzer Prize for Fiction winner, Edith Wharton

1923   Equal Rights Amendment introduced in Congress

1931   First woman Nobel Peace Prize winner, Jane Addams

1932   First woman to fly solo across the Atlantic, Amelia Earhart; first woman elected to U.S. Senate, Hattie Wyatt Caraway

1935   National Council of Negro Women founded

1938   Fair Labor Standards Act grants equal protection in the workplace

1941; 42   United States enters World War II; military accepts women in noncombat roles

1942   All American Girls Professional Baseball League begins

1948   United Nations adopts Universal Declaration of Human Rights

1961   John F. Kennedy forms President's Commission on the Status of Women

1963   Betty Friedan's *The Feminine Mystique* published

1966   National Organization for Women founded

1972   Title IX of the Education Act Amendments prohibits discrimination based on gender in federally assisted educational programs

1973   U.S. Supreme Court hears *Roe v. Wade* and legalizes abortion

1981   Wisconsin adopts a nondiscrimination law for lesbians and gay men, the first state to do so

1982   Equal Rights Amendment fails ratification

1990   First woman U.S. surgeon general, Antonia Novello

1993   First Take Our Daughters to Work Day

1997   First woman U.S. secretary of state, Madeleine Albright

2000   First First Lady to run for and win a political office, Hillary Rodham Clinton

SELECTED BIBLIOGRAPHY

Friedan, Betty. *Life So Far, a Memoir.* New York: Simon & Schuster, 2000.

Kendall, Martha E. *Susan B. Anthony: Voice for Women's Voting Rights.* Springfield, NJ: Enslow, 1997.

Lerner, Gerda. *The Female Experience: An American Documentary.* Indianapolis, IN: Bobbs-Merrill, 1977.

Owens-Adair, Bethenia. *Dr. Owens-Adair: Some of Her Life Experiences.* Portland, OR: Mann & Beach Printers, 1906.

Pipher, Mary. *Reviving Ophelia: Saving the Selves of Adolescent Girls.* New York: Ballantine, 1994.

Rappaport, Doreen. *American Women: Their Lives in Their Words.* New York: Thomas Crowell, 1990.

Rowbotham, Sheila. *A Century of Women: The History of Women in Britain and the United States.* New York: Viking, 1997.

Schlissel, Lillian. *Women's Diaries of the Westward Journey.* New York: Schocken, 1982.

Schneir, Miriam, ed. *Feminism: The Essential Historical Writings.* New York: Vintage, 1972.

Seller, Maxine Schwartz, ed. *Immigrant Women.* Philadelphia, PA: Temple University Press, 1981.

Spittal, William Guy, ed. *Iroquois Women: An Anthology.* Ontario, Canada: Iroqrafts, 1990.

Steinem, Gloria. *Moving beyond Words.* New York: Simon & Schuster, 1994.

Wise, Nancy Baker, and Christy Wise. *A Mouthful of Rivets: Women at Work in World War II.* San Francisco, CA: Jossey-Bass, 1994.

FURTHER READING FROM LERNER PUBLISHING GROUP

Ferris, Jeri. *Walking the Road to Freedom: A Story about Sojourner Truth.* Minneapolis, MN: Carolrhoda Books, Inc., 1988.

Galt, Margot Fortunato. *Up to the Plate: The All American Girls Professional Baseball League.* Minneapolis, MN: Lerner Publications Company, 1995.

Guernsey, JoAnn Bren. *Voices of Feminism: Past, Present, and Future.* Minneapolis, MN: Lerner Publications Company, 1996.

Josephson, Judith Pinkerton. *Mother Jones: Fierce Fighter for Workers' Rights.* Minneapolis, MN: Lerner Publications Company, 1997.

Krohn, Katherine. *Women of the Wild West.* Minneapolis, MN: Lerner Publications Company, 2000.

Lannin, Joanne. *A History of Basketball for Girls and Women: From Bloomers to Big Leagues.* Minneapolis, MN: Lerner Publications Company, 2000.

Lazo, Caroline. *Gloria Steinem: Feminist Extraordinaire.* Minneapolis, MN: Lerner Publications Company, 1998.

McPherson, Stephanie Sammartino. *Sisters against Slavery: A Story about Sarah and Angelina Grimké.* Minneapolis, MN: Carolrhoda Books, Inc., 1999.

Miller, Brandon Marie. *Buffalo Gals: Women of the Old West.* Minneapolis, MN: Lerner Publications Company, 1995.

Steiner, Andy. *A Sporting Chance: Sports and Gender.* Minneapolis, MN: Lerner Publications Company, 1995.

Swain, Gwenyth. *The Road to Seneca Falls: A Story about Elizabeth Cady Stanton.* Minneapolis, MN: Carolrhoda Books, Inc., 1996.

Wilson, Lori Lee. *The Salem Witch Trials.* Minneapolis, MN: Lerner Publications Company, 1997.

INDEX

abolition, 35–38, 40–41, 43, 46–47, 86
abortion, 71, 82–83
Adams, Abigail Smith, 18, 20–21
Adams, President John, 18, 20–21, 86
African American women, 73; Frances Ellen Watkins Harper, 47; intersection of civil and women's rights, 74–75; Harriet Tubman, 88; Ida B. Wells-Barnett, 89; Marian Anderson, 86; Prudence Crandall, 86; Shirley Chisholm, 81; and slavery, 33–35; Sojourner Truth, 43–44, 90; and Thirteenth Amendment, 47; and women's rights movement, 47
Albright, Madeleine, 83
Anderson, Marian, 86
Anthony, Susan B., 41, 44, 46, 53–54, 69, 87; and suffrage, 49–50, 53; and union organization, 47

Beauty Myth, The, 84
Beecher, Catharine, 28, 35
birth control, 58, 60–63, 66, 71, 86
Blackwell, Elizabeth, 87
Bloomer, Amelia, 44

Campbell, Flora, 30, 38
Catt, Carrie Chapman, 64, 68
children, 21–22, 31, 60, 74
children, custody of, 12, 33–34, 39, 40
Chisholm, Shirley, 81
civil rights movement, 74–75, 76
Clinton, President Bill, 83
Clinton, Hillary Rodham, 84
colonial women, 8–17
Comstock Laws, 58, 60
consciousness-raising groups, 79

Constitution, U.S.: Eighteenth Amendment to, 64, 71; and Equal Rights Amendment, 69, 79–81; First Amendment to, 21; Fourteenth Amendment to, 47; Nineteenth Amendment to, 64–65; Thirteenth Amendment to, 46–47; Crandall, Prudence, 86

Declaration of Independence, 20, 21, 39, 53
"Declaration of Sentiments," 38, 39, 40, 54
Doty, Faith, 13–14
Douglass, Frederick, 40, 58
Duniway, Abigail Scott, 49–50
Dyer, Mary Barret, 86

education: African American girls, 87; higher, 39, 46; and male domination, 27, 37; physical, 24, 59, 80; to prepare girls, 23–27; reform, 7, 41, 80, 84
Eighty Years and More, 29–30
Equal Rights Ammendment (ERA), 69–70, 79, 80–81, 91
excommunication, 14, 16, 20

fashion, 24, 27, 44; bloomers, 44, 59; bra burners, 80; flappers, 66; in media, 28–29, 84
Feminine Mystique, The, 77–78
feminists, 80, 84
Ferraro, Geraldine, 83
Friedan, Betty, 77, 81

Gage, Matilda Joslyn, 53
Gilman, Charlotte Perkins, 57
Grimké, Angelina, 35–37
Grimké, Sarah, 35–37

Harper, Frances Ellen Watkins, 47

Hibbens, Ann, 8
housewives, 8, 71–72, 73
Huerta, Dolores, 86
Hutchinson, Anne, 14–17, 21, 86

ideal woman: cult of true womanhood, 29, 43; flapper, 66; images from media, 28, 84; Miss America Beauty Pageant, 67–68; Puritan idea of femininity, 9; "true" woman, 66, 85
Incidents in the Life of a Slave Girl, 34

Jacobs, Harriet, 34, 35
Jones, Mary Harris (Mother Jones), 54–56

labor movement 32, 54–58, 73, 89
laws, protective, 12, 20, 68–69
Lockwood, Belva, 87

Mankiller, Wilma, 83
marriage: colonial 8, 10–12; and education, 28; and keeping maiden name, 46; market of 22, 27; preparation for, 23–24; and property, right to own, 46; sex and childbirth, 58, 60, 61; and workplace, 23, 32, 57, 70, 88
Mayer, Maria Goeppert, 87
motherhood, 60, 61, 68
mothers, 10, 24–25, 50, 67, 74
Mott, Lucretia, 39, 40
Murray, Judith Sargent, 26, 28
My Fight for Birth Control, 60

Narrative of the Life of Mrs. Mary Jemison, A, 22
Nation, Carry, 51–52
National Woman Suffrage Association, 47, 53–54, 63, 91

Native American women,
21–22, 83, 86, 88

O'Connor, Sandra Day, 87

Parks, Rosa, 75
Paul, Alice, 63, 68, 69
pioneers, 48–49
Planned Parenthood, 60, 71
political office, women in, 58,
81, 83
political participation, women's,
21, 35–36, 47
professions, 68, 74; women's
exclusion from, 7, 22, 26, 30,
39, 46; women's right to
enter, 27, 57; women in
male-dominated, 48, 49–50,
84, 86–88
property, owning, 11–14, 21,
30, 46
Puritans, 8, 9, 14, 15, 86

religion: and birth control, 58,
63, 71; and division of roles,
11, 46; excommunication, 14,
16, 20; freedom of, 14, 16,
86; and girls' education, 23;
and government, 14, 16, 21,
36; and temperance
movement, 51
Ride, Sally, 88
rights, women's: to be elected to
political office, 21, 40, see
also political office, women
in; to childcare, 84; to
control own sexuality, 58,
60–61, 82; to custody of
children, 7, 12, 33–34, 39,
40; to equal athletic
opportunities, 7, 59, 80; to
equal education, 7, 30, see
also education; to equal
employment (see workplace);
to equal pay (see wages);
freedom from violence, 12; as
human rights, 84; to own

property, 7, 11–14, 40–41,
87, see also property, owning;
to sign contracts, 7, 11,
13–14, 37; to speak publicly,
7; to vote (see suffrage,
woman)
role, woman's, 11, 63, 75, 81

Sampson, Deborah, 19–20
Sanger, Margaret Higgins,
60–63, 71
Schlafly, Phyllis, 80
segregation, 39, 73, 75
Seneca Falls convention, 39–41,
49, 53, 65, 90
single women, 9, 11, 23–24, 41,
53, 57, 81
slavery, 86; African American
women and, 33–35; white
women and, 36–37
Stanton, Elizabeth Cady, 44, 69,
87; activism, 38–42, 46–47,
53–54, 65; "true" woman, 66,
85; women's right to own
property, 29–30
Steinem, Gloria, 79, 85
Stone, Lucy, 45–46
suffrage, woman, 7, 52, 56, 58,
63; U.S. Constitution, 46–47,
64–65; and western states,
49–50. See also Seneca Falls
convention

temperance movement, 39, 41,
47, 51–52, 64, 71
Title VII, 76–77, 78
Title IX of the Education
Amendments of 1972, 7, 80
Troy Female Seminary, 25–26,
38, 90
Truth, Sojourner, 43–44, 90
Tubman, Harriet, 88

unions, 32, 54–58, 73
United Nations Fourth
International Conference on
Women, 84

wages: and Great Depression,
70; low, 22, 30–32, 68, 88;
unequal, 7, 39, 57, 85; and
World War II, 71–74. See also
labor movement; professions
Waight, Lavinia, 30, 32
Wells-Barnett, Ida B., 89
widows, 12, 23, 30, 31, 54
Willard, Emma, 25–26, 38
Willard, Frances, 52
Wilson, President Woodrow,
63–64, 69
Winthrop, Governor John,
16–17
witches and witchcraft, 8–9
Wolf, Naomi, 84
Wollstonecraft, Mary, 24, 25,
28, 90
women's rights, resistance to, 36,
44–45, 50
women's rights movement: and
abolition movement, 36–37
38–39, 41, 43, 46–47; after
woman suffrage, 68; and civil
rights movement, 74–75;
conventions, 39–47; and
ERA, 68–70; and
government, 21; and labor
movement, 56–57, 68; and
pioneers, 49; and pro-choice
movement, 58; second wave,
77; and temperance
movement, 41, 47, 52; as
women's liberation movement,
78–80
Woodhull, Victoria, 58, 61
workplace: discrimination in,
76–77, 84–85; protective
laws, 68–69; reform of, 41,
47, 54–58, 88; World War I,
63–64, 66; World War II,
71–74. See also professions;
wages; labor movement
Wright, Frances, 27, 28, 86

Zaharias, Mildred "Babe"
Didrikson, 89

ACKNOWLEDGMENTS

Photographs and illustrations used with permission of: Brown Brothers, pp. 2–3, 42, 56, 62, 65; © Corbis, pp. 6, 25, 33, 45, 48; © Bettmann/Corbis, pp. 8, 37, 38, 52, 57, 66, 76, 78, 79, 81; North Wind Picture Archives, pp. 9, 10, 12, 28, 29, 31, 64; © Culver Pictures, p. 13; Library of Congress, pp. 15, 18, 26, 36 (both), 43, 46, 49, 53, 59; Archive Photos, pp. 19, 22, 68; detail of *The Graham Children* by William Hogarth, Tate Gallery, London, p. 23; North Carolina Division of Archives and History, p. 35; The Newberry Library, p. 55; National Archives, p. 72; The Hoover Company, North Canton, Ohio, p. 74; Reuters/Terry Bochatey/Archive Photos, p. 82; Cherokee Nation of Oklahoma, p. 83 (left); Reuters/Rick Wilking/Archive Photos, p. 83 (right); Reuters/Will Burgess/Archive Photos, p. 85.

Front cover: Brown Brothers
Back cover: National Archives (W&C # 798)
Cover design by Zachary Marell

LERNER'S AWARD-WINNING PEOPLE'S HISTORY SERIES:

Accept No Substitutes! The History of American Advertising

Buffalo Gals: Women of the Old West

Dressed for the Occasion: What Americans Wore 1620–1970

Failure Is Impossible! The History of American Women's Rights

Farewell, John Barleycorn: Prohibition in the United States

Get Up and Go: The History of American Road Travel

Just What the Doctor Ordered: The History of American Medicine

Slave Young, Slave Long: The American Slave Experience

Snapshot: America Discovers the Camera

Stop This War! American Protest of the Conflict in Vietnam

This Land Is Your Land: The American Conservation Movement

Uncle Sam Wants You: The Military Men and Women of World War II

V Is for Victory: The American Home Front during World War II

We Have Marched Together: The Working Children's Crusade

What's Cooking? The History of American Food

When This Cruel War Is Over: The Civil War Home Front

For more information, please call 1-800-328-4929 or visit www.lernerbooks.com.